Jokes from the Internet

Everyone has a photographic memory. Some don't have film.

Other Books by Fred Ward

DIAMONDS
DIAMONDS (in Russian)
EMERALDS
GEM CARE
JADE
JADES OF MESOAMERICA
OPALS
PEARLS
RUBIES & SAPPHIRES

GOLDEN ISLANDS OF THE CARIBBEAN
INSIDE CUBA TODAY
PORTRAIT OF A PRESIDENT

Books by Charlotte and Fred Ward

THE HOME BIRTH BOOK

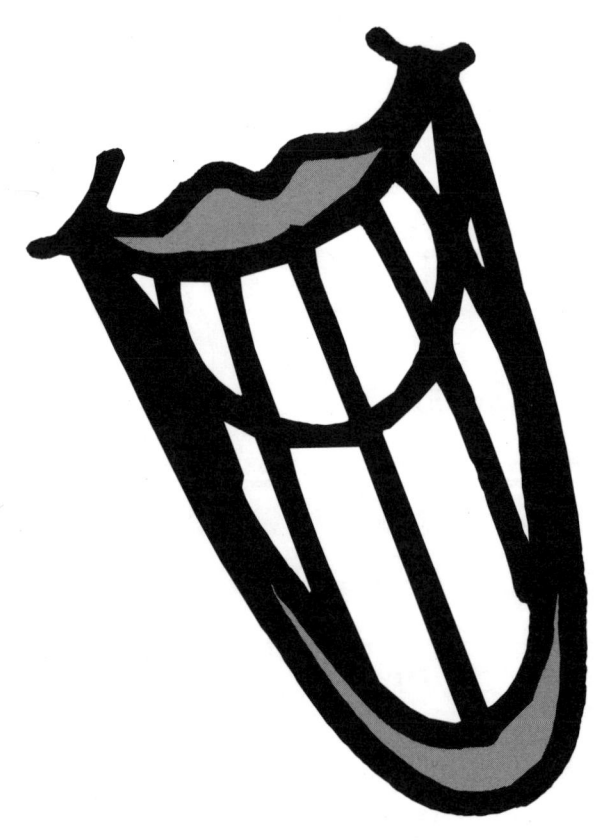

Jokes from the Internet

Fred Ward (signature)

Fred Ward

Gem Book Publishers
7106 Saunders Court
Bethesda, MD 20817

Copyright © 1999 Fred Ward

All rights reserved. No part of this book may be reproduced in any form or by any electronic or mechanical means, including information storage and retrieval systems, without written permission from the publisher, except by a reviewer who may quote brief passages in a review. This book includes images from *Corel Mega Gallery* that are protected by the copyright laws of the U.S., Canada, and elsewhere. Used under license.

Acknowledgments:

Many generous people make a project such as this possible. A compilation of contemporary jokes depends on the contributions of many humorous folks. The Internet is filled with jokes and stories, hundreds daily in fact, but sorting through them is too much for any single person. So I owe a debt of gratitude to many of my friends who continue to filter through the daily NET influx and pass on to me only those jokes they feel are worthy. Assembling jokes and cartoons into a sensible, attractive, and readable form took months of work and an orderly plan. Locating artwork and then brilliantly matching appropriate images to each joke became the task of Michele Zabel, who viewed hundreds of thousands of drawings to choose these nine hundred. Charise Petrovitch provided assistance with clip art. Charlotte Ward's editing talents brought grammatical order and style to the chaotic raw material from the Internet.

In addition to regularly checking dozens of Internet joke sites, I relied on individual contributors for the majority of jokes printed here. Among these generous jokesters are: Nancy and Steve Attaway, David Austen, Tom Banker, Jeffrey Bergman, Pete and Hunt Brand, Jim and Lynn Erckmann, Martin Fuller, Bruce and Cathy Gaber, Bill Garrett, Dick Hughes, Anne Jamison, Mark Jones, Kirk Makepeace, Jimilu Mason, Doug Parsons, Ken Penland, Mary Smith, John Smith, and Bo Torrey. To all, a heartfelt thanks!

F.W.

Published by Gem Book Publishers
7106 Saunders Court
Bethesda, MD 20817 USA
Telephone 301-983-1990
FAX 301-983-3980

http://www.erols.com/fward/
fward@erols.com

First edition, 1999

ISBN 1-887651-03-9

The Genesis of
Jokes From The Internet

A man walks into a computer store and hands a clerk a floppy disk.
He asks, "Will you put the Internet on this for me?"

The Internet is today's water cooler, the place to pick up the latest story or laugh. Once I began logging onto the NET some years ago, I noticed that the two most prevalent activities were exchanging email messages and sharing jokes. Both forms of communications have grown exponentially. I realized the NET had become the most popular joke distribution system in history when I began receiving the same joke six or more times during a single day. The speed with which jokes make the round-the-world circuit multiple times surely is faster than the Space Shuttle and must be near the speed of light. (*George Carlin asks, "Ever wonder what's the speed of dark?"*)

Once I started saving jokes for my own amusement, I began sharing them with friends on the NET. It was only a small step from there to the idea of creating a book. I have nine books on gemstones currently in print (and four books on other subjects out of print), so adding another title seemed relatively easy. I had only a slight comprehension of the magnitude of the task. With my gem books I personally gather all the information. With this book the jokes arrived in up to three hundred emails a day! Clearly, I had to organize jokes to eliminate duplicate, gross, and unfunny ones. As a visual person I knew the new joke book had to be filled with graphics. Soon fifteen hundred carefully selected cartoon images consumed a hard disk of their own. Slowly this book project took shape as designing these pages became a joyful way to spend each day.

Nothing is as ethereal or anonymous as a joke. Jokes appear, seemingly from nowhere and from everywhere. They have a life of their own. They flit and fly into almost every home and office in the world, and then they disappear. For the most part, the jokes arrived just as I share them with you here. But who writes them? It appears that no one knows who the authors are. Few seem to take credit for the jokes that move around the globe daily. When I knew the authors, I gave credit.

One other policy I followed here was to change names in funny news items. I have no way to check if those named people actually did the things that were reported in the newspapers quoted. So I kept the stories I found amusing and altered the names.

I sincerely hope you find many funny things in this book. If you have new funny stories or jokes, please use my email address at the front of the book to share them with me. I view this edition as a beginning, the first of an Internet joke book series. Sharing your jokes with me and others will make a new edition a reality.

Thanks. Now enjoy some good laughs.

F.W.

I brake for no apparent reason.

Out of my mind; back in five minutes.

I took an I.Q. test, and the results were negative.

Earth First! We'll strip-mine the other planets later.

Where there's a will, I want to be in it.

If we are what we eat, I'm cheap, fast, and easy.

All generalizations are false, including this one.

CONTENTS

Animals	11
Blonde Jokes	21
Bumper Stickers	31
Celebrities	35
Computers & Technology	47
Corporate America	59
Drinking	67
Education	75
Ethnic Jokes	81
Government	87
Henny Youngman	93
Kids' Jokes	99
Lawyer Jokes	109
Medical Jokes	117
Men	125
Miscellaneous	137
Movies	143
News	151
Office Jokes	163
Philosophy	173
Quotes From Dan Quayle	183
Rednecks & Cowboys	187
Relationships	195
Religious Jokes	203
Scientists & Engineers	213
Senior Citizens Jokes	219
Sex Jokes	227
Sports Jokes	239
Women	245

Outside of a dog,
a book is
man's best friend.
Inside of a dog,
it's too dark
to read.

Groucho Marx

ANIMALS

Alligator Shoes...

An army ranger was on vacation in the depths of Louisiana. He wanted a pair of genuine alligator shoes in the worst way but was reluctant to pay the high prices the local vendors were asking.

After becoming very frustrated with the "no haggle" attitude of one of the shopkeepers, the ranger shouted, "Maybe I'll just go out and get my own alligator so I can have a pair of shoes made at a reasonable price!"

The vendor said, "By all means, be my guest. Maybe you'll run into a couple of marines who were in here earlier saying the same thing."

So the ranger headed into the bayou. A few hours later he came upon two men standing waist deep in water. He thought, "They must be the two marines the guy in town was talking about."

Just then the ranger saw a tremendously long gator swimming rapidly toward one of the men. As the gator was about to attack, the marine grabbed its neck with both hands and strangled it to death with very little effort. Then both marines dragged it on shore near several other dead gators.

Once they got it flipped on its back, one of the marines exclaimed, "Damn, this one doesn't have any shoes either!"

Dog Property Laws...

If it's mine, it must never appear to be yours in any way.
If I'm chewing something up, all the pieces are mine.
If you're playing with something and you put it down,
it's automatically mine.
If I like it, it's mine.
If it's in my mouth, it's mine.
If I can take it from you, it's mine.
If I had it a little while ago, it's mine.
If it just looks like mine, it's mine.
If I saw it first, it's mine.

If it's broken, it's yours.

Blind As A Bat...

A vampire bat covered in fresh blood came flapping in from the night and parked himself on the roof of the cave to sleep. Pretty soon all the other bats smelled the blood and began hassling him about where he got it. He told them to knock it off and let him sleep, but they persisted until finally he gave in.

"OK, follow me," he said and flew out of the cave with hundreds of bats behind him. Down through the valley they went, across the river, and into the forest.

Finally he slowed down, and all the other bats excitedly milled around him.

"Now, do you see that tree over there?" he asked.

"Yes, yes, yes!" the bats all screamed in a frenzy.

"Good," said the first bat, "Because I DIDN'T!"

Panda Pun Fun...

A panda walked into a bar, and the bartender asked what he'd like. The panda asked if he had any bamboo. The barkeep said he had only the little bamboo umbrellas to put into fancy drinks. The Panda asked if the umbrellas were expensive and was told he could have them for a good price. They agreed on six for a dollar. The panda drew up a barstool, paid, and ate all the little umbrellas.

He then got off the stool, pulled out two six-guns, and proceeded to shoot the hell out of the place. The barman dove for the floor. When he stood up after the smoke had cleared, he saw the panda had gone. Grabbing a dictionary, he read:

"*Panda*: Eats bamboo shoots and leaves."

Ship Away...

A spinster and a sailor's parrot were the only survivors of a shipwreck. They'd been clinging to a piece of driftwood for days. "How's your wrinkled old ass?" croaked the parrot.

"Oh, shut up!" snapped the old maid.

"Mine, too," said the parrot. "Must be this saltwater."

Smart Chicks Want To Know...

A baby chick was having a heart-to-heart talk with its mother.
"Am I people?" he asked.
"No," replied the mama, "you're a chicken."
"Do chickens come from people?"
 "No, chickens come from eggs."
  "Are eggs born?"
   "No, eggs are laid."
    "Are people laid?"
     "Not all—
      some are chicken."

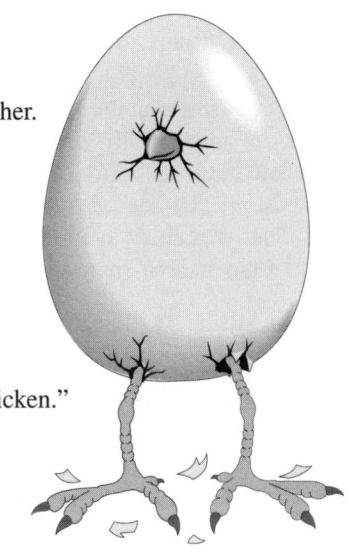

What Else Can He Do?

A mangy looking guy comes into a restaurant and orders food. The waiter says, "I don't think you can pay." The guy says, "You're right. I don't have any money, but if I show you something inredible you've never seen before, will you give me some food?"

"You've got a deal!"

The guy reaches into his coat pocket and pulls out a hamster. He puts it onto the counter. It jumps off the end, runs across the room, climbs up the piano, leaps onto the keyboard, and starts playing Gershwin. This hamster is good!

The waiter says, "You're right. I've never seen anything like him before. Your hamster is really good." The guy downs the hamburger he had ordered and asks for another. "Money or another miracle," replies the waiter. The guy reaches into his coat again and pulls out a frog. He puts the frog onto the counter, and the frog starts to sing. It has a marvelous voice and great pitch. This frog is good!

A stranger from the other end of the counter runs over to the guy and offers him $300 for the frog. The guy says, "It's a deal." He takes the money and gives the stranger the frog.

As the stranger runs out of the restaurant, the waiter says to the guy, "Are you crazy? You sold a singing frog for $300? It must be worth millions."

"Not so," says the guy, "the hamster is also a ventriloquist."

With Just A Hint Of Whale...

One beautiful autumn day a park ranger discovered a man sitting in the woods chewing away on a dead bald eagle.

"Hey, mister, the bald eagle is a protected species, so killing one is a punishable offense," said the ranger.

He swiftly arrested the man and ushered him before a judge.

In court the man pleaded innocent to the charges against him, claiming that if he hadn't eaten the eagle, he would have starved to death.

"I was so hungry," complained the defensive camper. "The bald eagle was the only food I could find!"

To everyone's amazement, the judge ruled in favor of the man.

In the judge's closing statement he asked the man, "I would like you to tell me something before I let you go. I have never eaten a bald eagle and don't plan to. But I'd like to know. What did it taste like?"

The man answered, "You'd probably like it. Bald eagle tastes like a cross between whooping crane and spotted owl."

Where do you get Virgin Wool?
Ugly sheep!

What did the fish say when he hit the concrete wall?
Dam!!

A sign at a Victoria Falls crocodile farms states: "Any person throwing litter into the crocodile pens will be asked to retrieve it."

Forget The Exam, Let's Scan...

A man carrying his dog runs screaming for help into the vet's office. The vet rushes him back to an examining room and has him lay his dog on a table. The vet examines the limp body and after a few moments tells the man that, regrettably, his dog is dead.

Clearly agitated and unwilling to accept this news, the man demands a second opinion. The vet goes into the back room and comes out with a cat. He sets the cat next to the dog's body. The cat walks from head to tail sniffing the dog's body and finally looks at the vet and meows. The vet turns to the man and says, "I'm sorry, but the cat thinks your dog is dead."

The man is still unwilling to believe his dog is dead. The vet brings in a black Labrador retriever. The Lab sniffs the body, walks from head to tail, and finally looks at the vet and barks. The vet looks at the man and says, "I'm sorry, but the Lab thinks your dog is dead."

Finally, resigned to the diagnosis, the man thanks the vet and asks how much he owes. The vet answers, "$650."

"What? $650 to tell me my dog is dead?" exclaims the man.

"Well," the vet replies, "I would only have charged you $50 for my initial diagnosis. The additional $600 is for the CAT scan and Lab test."

You Are A Frog Of Many Parts...

A lonely frog telephones the Psychic Hotline to ask what his future holds. His Personal Psychic Advisor says, "You're going to meet a beautiful young girl who will want to know everything about you."

"Great! I'm thrilled!" the frog replies.
"Will I meet her at a party?"

"No," says the psychic, "in a biology class."

The Dwarf And The Horse...

A dwarf with a lisp goes to an agricultural show to buy a mare. He wanders around until he comes across a beautiful mare inside a small enclosure with a farmer standing at the gate. He goes up to the farmer and says, "Excthuth me, may I have a look at your horth?"

"Sure," says the farmer, "come on in."

The dwarf wanders round and round the mare and then stops. He says to the farmer, "Her eyeth, her eyeth, I want to see her eyeth."

The farmer has to bend down to pick up the dwarf to show him the mare's eyes.

"Nith eyeth, nith eyeth, I like thith horth, I like thith horth, I think I want to buy thith horth."

Once again the dwarf wanders around the horse, in turn asking the farmer to pick him up to show him the mare's ears and then exclaiming, "Nith earth, nith earth, I like thith horth, I like thith horth, I think I want to buy thith horth."

The farmer is starting to get pissed off because the dwarf is quite heavy.

Suddenly the dwarf stops in his tracks and says, "Her twat. her twat, I want to see her twat!"

The farmer, infuriated, pick up the dwarf and drives him head first into the mare's rear.

After watching the little legs kick for a long minute, the farmer extracts the dwarf from his predicament.

The dwarf wipes himself down and says. "I think I better wephrase that... I'd like to thee her gallop!"

MY DOG CAN LICK ANYONE.

I love cats ...
they taste just like chicken.

And In Alaska...

If you are camping in Alaska this summer, please note the following public service announcement:

Use caution on the trail. Watch out for bears. When hiking in bear country, wear tiny bells on your clothes. Bells scare away MOST bears (grizzly, black, etc.).

Please note that bells do not frighten Kodiak bears. To help alert you to the presence of Kodiak bears, pay particular attention to bear droppings.

One can easily spot Kodiak bear droppings. They are the droppings that contain those tiny bells.

Why don't they just make mouse-flavored cat food?

Husband and cat lost! Reward for cat.

Shoot The Chihuahua...

This guy wakes up one morning to find a gorilla in his tree. He finds a gorilla removal service in the phone book.

"Is it a male or female gorilla?" the service guy asks. "Male," is the man's response. "Oh yeah, I can do it. I'll be right there." says the service guy.

An hour later the service guy shows up with a stick, a Chihuahua, a shotgun, and a pair of hand cuffs. He proceeds to give the man instructions. "I'm going to climb this tree and poke the gorilla with the stick until he falls. When he does, the trained Chihuahua will bite off his testicles. The gorilla will then cross his hands to protect himself, which will give you a chance to snap on the handcuffs." The man asks, "What do I do with the shotgun?"

"If I fall out of the tree before the gorilla, shoot the Chihuahua."

The Great Dog Fight...

The Americans and Russians at the height of the arms race realized if they continued in the usual manner, they were going to blow up the whole world.

One day they sat down and decided to settle their entire dispute with one dog fight. They would have five years to breed the best fighting dog in the world. Whichever dog won would entitle its side to dominate the world. The losing side would have to lay down its arms.

The Russians found the biggest meanest Doberman and Rottweiler bitches in the world and bred them with the biggest meanest Siberian wolves. They selected only the biggest strongest puppy from each litter and killed his siblings so that he would get all the milk. They used steroids and trainers and after five years the Russians came up with the biggest meanest dog the world had ever seen. It needed five-inch-thick steel bars on its cage. Nobody dared go near.

When the day came for the fight, the Americans showed up with a strange-looking animal. It was a nine-foot-long dachshund. All the observers felt sorry for the Americans because they knew their entry could not last 10 seconds against the Russian dog.

When the cages were opened, the dachshund came out of it's cage and slowly waddled over towards the Russian dog. Snarling, the Russian dog leaped out of its cage and charged the American dachshund. But just as it was about to bite the dachshund's neck, the dachshund opened it's mouth and consumed the Russian dog in one bite. There was nothing left at all of the Russian dog.

The Russians came up to the Americans shaking their heads in disbelief. "We don't understand how this could have happened. We had our best people working five years with the meanest Doberman and Rottweiler bitches in the world and the biggest meanest Siberian wolves."

"That's nothing," the American team leader thought to himself. "We had our best plastic surgeons working five years to make an alligator look like a dachshund."

How To Succeed—For A While...

A pheasant was standing in a field chatting to a bull. "I would love to be able to get to the top of yonder tree," sighed the pheasant, "but I don't have the energy." "Well, why don't you nibble on some of my droppings?" replied the bull. "They're packed with nutrients." After the pheasant had pecked at a lump of dung, it found enough strength to reach the first branch of the tree.

The next day, after eating more dung, it reached the second branch. After the fourth night it proudly perched at the top of the tree.

Whereupon, a farmer spotted it, dashed into the farmhouse, and emerged with a shotgun. He shot that pheasant right out of the tree.

Moral of the Story:
Bullshit might get you to the top, but it won't keep you there.

Wanna See A Goat Fly?

Two guys are walking through the woods when they come across this big deep hole. "Wow, that looks deep." "Sure does. Let's throw in something to see how deep it is." They throw in some pebbles and wait. No sound. "Jeeez. That is REALLY deep. Here, throw one of these great big rocks down there. It should make a noise."

They pick up a couple of football-sized rocks and throw them into the hole, and wait, and wait. Nothing. They look at each other in amazement. One gets a determined look on his face and says, "Hey, over in the weeds there's a railroad tie. Help me carry it. When we throw THAT sucker in, it's GOTTA make noise." The two drag the heavy tie over to the hole and heave it in. Not a sound comes from the hole.

Suddenly, out of the nearby woods a goat appears running like the wind. It rushes toward the two men, then right past them as fast as it's legs will carry it. Without stopping, it flies through the air and into the hole.

The two men are astonished at what they've seen. Out of the woods comes a farmer, who spots the men and ambles over. "Hey, you two guys seen my goat?" "You bet we did! Wildest thing I've ever seen! It came running like crazy and jumped into this hole!" "Nah," says the farmer, "That couldn't have been MY goat. My goat was chained to a railroad tie."

Why did the blonde get fired from the M&M factory? She kept throwing out the "W's"!

Blonde Jokes

That's Some Stroke...

A blonde competed with a brunette and a redhead in the breast stroke division of the women's English Channel swim competition. The brunette came in first and the redhead second. The blonde came in last. She said,
"I'm usually not one to complain, but I think they used their arms!"

Think About It...

Q: How do you know a blonde has been on your computer?
A: There's whiteout on the screen.

Q: How do you know another blonde has been on your computer?
A: There's writing over the whiteout.

Q: How is a blonde like a turtle?
A: When they're on their backs, they're both screwed!

Q: Why don't blondes in San Francisco wear mini-skirts?
A: Because their balls would show.

Q: Why do blonde women have bruises around their belly buttons?
A: Blonde men aren't too smart either.

She Was So Blonde...

....she spent 20 minutes looking at the orange juice carton, which read "concentrate."
....she put lipstick on her forehead because she wanted to make up her mind.
....she told me to meet her at the corner of "WALK" and "DON'T WALK."
....she thought TuPac Shakur was a Jewish holiday.
....she tried to put M&Ms in alphabetical order.
....she sat on the TV and watched the couch.
....she sent me a fax with a stamp on it.
....she tried to drown a fish.
....she thought a quarterback was a refund.
....she got locked in a grocery store and starved to death.
....if you gave her a penny for intelligence, you'd get back change.
....they had to burn down the school to get her out of third grade.
....under "Education" on her job application, she put "Hooked On Phonics."
....she tripped over a cordless phone.
....she took a ruler to bed to see how long she slept.
....at the bottom of the application, where it said "Sign Here," she put "Sagittarius."
....she asked for a price check at the Dollar Store.
....it took her two hours to watch 60 Minutes.
....if she spoke her mind, she'd probably be speechless.
....she studied for a blood test—and failed.
....she thought Boyz II Men was a day-care center.
....she thought Meow Mix was a record for cats.
....she thought she needed a token to get on Soul Train.
....she got stabbed in a shootout.
....she sold the car for gas money.

....when she saw "NC-17" (under 17 not admitted), she went home to get 16 friends.
....when she heard that 90 percent of all crimes occur around the home, she moved.
....she thinks Taco Bell is where you pay your phone bill.
....when she missed the #44 bus, she took the #22 bus twice instead.
....on the way to the airport, when she saw a sign that said "Airport Left," she turned around and went home.

And Still More Blondes

What's the difference between a prostitute, a nymphomaniac, and a blonde?
The prostitute says "Aren't you done yet?" The nympho says "Are you done already?" The blonde says "Beige... I think I'll have the ceiling painted beige."

What's the difference between a blonde and a limousine?
Not everybody has been in a limo.

Why do blondes like tilt steering?
More head room.

How do you keep a blonde busy?
Write "Please turn over" on both sides of a piece of paper.

How do you keep a blonde in suspense?
(I'll tell you tomorrow.)

What's the first thing a blonde does in the morning?
Puts her clothes on and goes home.

How does a blonde turn on the light?
She opens the car door.

What does a blonde call safe sex?
Padded headboards.

What do you call a dead blonde in a closet?
The 1992 World Hide-and-Seek Champion.

Why did Sherwin Williams name their new paint color "Blonde?"
Because it's not too bright, and it's easy to spread.

What's the difference between blondes and traffic signs?
Some traffic signs say "Stop."

What goes "VROOOM... SCREECH VROOOM... SCREECH VROOOM... SCREECH?"
A blonde at a flashing red light.

What does a blonde say when you ask her if her blinker is on?
"It's on. It's off. It's on. It's off. It's on. It's off."

What does a blonde answer to the question "Are you sexually active?"
"No, I just lie there."

What is the blonde's chronic speech impediment?
She can't say "No."

What did the blonde customer say to the buxom waitress (reading her name tag)?
"'Debbie' ... that's cute. What do you call the other one?"

What's the difference between a blonde and a mosquito?
A mosquito stops sucking when you slap it.

What's the difference between a blonde and a shopping cart?
Shopping carts sometimes seem to have minds of their own.

How do you make a blonde's eyes light up?
Shine a flashlight in her ear.

What did the blonde say when the doctor told her she was pregnant?
"Is it mine?"

What did the blonde say to her cyber-lover when he said he had love handles?
"Oh, that's OK. I love a man with cute ears."

What did the blonde say when she first saw Cheerios?
"Oh, look! Doughnut seeds."

What's special about the new "Blonde Barbi?"
You put a ring on its finger and its hips expand.

What is the mating call of the blonde?
"Ohh, I'm soooo drunk!"

How do you measure a blonde's IQ?
With a tire gauge.

A brunette says: "Oh, there's a dead bird!"
The blonde looks up and says, "Where?"

What does the blonde yell in an emergency? What's the number for 911!

Ever heard of a suicide blonde? Dyed by her own hands.

Why don't blondes eat pickles?
They can't get their head into the jar!

How do you tell if a blonde is a good cook?
She gets the Pop Tarts out of the toaster in one piece.

When a blonde ordered a pizza, the clerk asked if she wanted it cut into 6 or 12 slices. The blonde said that she could never eat 12!

A blonde got very depressed when she looked at her driver's license and noticed that she gotten an "F" in sex!

Why can't blondes be pharmacists?
They can't get the bottles into the typewriter!

What's a blonde doing when she grasps at thin air?
Collecting her thoughts!

Why did the blonde climb the glass wall?
To see what was on the other side!

Blondes Will Listen To Men In Uniforms...

A blonde gets on an airplane and sits down in the first-class section. The stewardess tells her she must move to coach because she doesn't have a first-class ticket. The blonde replies, "I'm blonde, I'm smart, and I have a good job, so I'm staying in first class until we reach Jamaica." The stewardess gets the head stewardess, who then asks the woman to leave. Again the woman says, "I'm blonde, I'm smart, I have a good job, so I'm staying in first class until we reach Jamaica."

The stewardesses don't know what to do because they have to seat the rest of the passengers before takeoff, so they call for the copilot. The copilot leans close to the blonde and whispers into her ear. She immediately gets up and goes to her seat in the coach section. Puzzled, the lead stewardess asks the copilot what he said to get her to move. The copilot replies, "I told her the front half of the airplane wasn't going to Jamaica."

Waiting For Three Cherries...

A blonde heading for a soda machine arrived just before a businessman coming to quench his thirst. She took 50 cents from her purse, inserted the coins, studied the selections, pushed the button for Diet Coke, and out came a Diet Coke, which she placed on a counter by the machine. Then she reached into her purse again, pulled out a dollar, and inserted it into the machine. Studying the choices carefully, she pushed the button for Coke Classic, and out came a Coke Classic with 50 cents change. She immediately took the 50 cents and put it into the machine, studied it for a moment, and pushed the Mountain Dew button. Out came a Mountain Dew.

As she was reaching into her purse again, the business man who had been waiting patiently for several minutes now spoke up. "Excuse me, Miss, but are you done yet?"

She looked at him and replied indignantly: "Well, Duhhh, not while I'm still winning!"

Check The Roots...

A brunette goes into a doctor's office.

Brunette: "Doctor, I don't know what's wrong with me."
Doctor: "Tell me your symptoms."
Brunette: "Well, everything hurts. When I touch my nose, it hurts (touching nose), when I touch my leg, it hurts (touching leg), when I touch my arm, it hurts (touching arm). It hurts everywhere!"
Doctor (after looking at her for a second): "Did you used to be a blonde?"
Brunette: "Why yes!"
Doctor: "You have a broken finger."

Really Short-Term Memory...

A blonde with two red ears went to the doctor. The doctor asked her what had happened to her ears, and she answered, "I was ironing a shirt and the phone rang—but instead of picking up the phone, I accidentally picked up the iron and stuck it to my ear."

"Oh Dear!" the doctor exclaimed in disbelief. "But...what happened to your other ear?"

"The son of a bitch called back."

Any Last Words???

Three women are about to be executed; a brunette, a redhead, and a blonde.

After the guard brings the brunette forward, the executioner asks if she has any last requests. She says no, and the executioner shouts, "Ready!...Aim!! ..."

Suddenly the brunette yells, "EARTHQUAKE!!!" Startled, everyone looks around, and she escapes.

Then the guard brings the redhead forward. The executioner asks if she has any last requests. She say no, and the executioner shouts, "Ready! ... Aim!!..."

Suddenly the redhead yells, "TORNADO!!!" Startled, everyone looks around, and she escapes.

By now the blonde has it all figured out. The guard brings her forward, and the executioner asks if she has any last requests. She says no. So the executioner shouts, "Ready! ... Aim!! ..."

...and the blonde yells, "FIRE!!!"

The Blonde Stewardess...

An airline captain had on board a very pretty new blonde stewardess. The route they were flying had a stopover in another city. So upon arrival the captain showed the stewardess the best place for airline personnel to eat, shop, and overnight.

The next morning as the pilot was preparing the crew for the day's route, he noticed the new stewardess was missing. He called her to find out what had happened. She answered the phone, sobbing, saying she couldn't get out of her room.

"You can't get out of your room?" the captain asked, "Why not?" The stewardess replied: "There are only three doors in here," she cried. "One's the bathroom, one's the closet, and one has a sign on it that says 'Do Not Disturb'!"

The Pearly Gates...

Three blondes die and go to Heaven. At the Pearly Gates, St. Peter tells them they may enter if they can answer one simple question.

St. Peter asks the first blonde, "What is Easter?"

The blonde replies, "Oh, that's easy! It's the holiday in November when everyone gets together, eats turkey, and acts thankful."

"Wrong!," replies St. Peter and proceeds to ask the second blonde the same question, "What is Easter?"

The second blonde replies, "Easter is the holiday in December when we put up a nice tree, exchange presents, and celebrate the birth of Jesus."

St. Peter looks at the second blonde, shakes his head in disgust, and tells her she's wrong. Then peering over his glasses at the third blonde, he asks, "What is Easter?"

Smiling confidently, the third blonde calmly tells St. Peter, "I know what Easter is."

Oh?" says St. Peter, incredulously.

She begins, "Easter is the Christian holiday that coincides with the Jewish celebration of Passover. Jesus and his disciples ate the Last Supper. Judas, one of his disciples, betrayed Jesus with a kiss. The Romans made Jesus wear a crown of thorns. They took him to be crucified, where he was nailed to a cross and stabbed in the side. He was buried in a nearby cave, which was sealed off by a large boulder."

St. Peter smiles broadly with delight.

The third blonde continues, "Every year the boulder is moved aside so that Jesus can come out... and, if he sees his shadow, we will have six more weeks of winter."

Two Cubes Short Of A Full Tray...

One day a man comes home from work to find his blonde wife leaning over the kitchen sink crying. He says, "Honey, what's wrong?" She says between sniffles, "I... I dropped the ice cubes on the floor, so I rinsed them off in hot water. Now I can't find them."

Why don't blondes like to make Kool Aid?
They can't fit all of the water
into the package!

WHY DO BLONDES WEAR PONYTAILS? TO HIDE THE VALVE STEM!

Why don't you let blondes take coffee breaks?
It takes too long to retrain them!

How do you tell if a blonde writes mysteries? She has a checkbook!

How may blondes does it take to change a light bulb?
Only one, but she gets six hours of college credit!

Blonde And Colorful...

A blonde, a brunette, and a redhead all tried out for the same job as a road striper. The boss told them that after three days, whoever had painted the longest line would get the job.

At the end of the first day the redhead had painted 3 miles, the brunette had painted 2.5 miles, and the blonde had painted 10 miles. The boss got so exited he told her to keep it up and the job was hers. The next day when the redhead painted 5 miles and the brunette 5.6 miles and the blonde only 4 miles, he told the blonde not to worry because she still had a good lead.

On the third day the redhead painted 6 miles, the brunette 5 miles, and the blonde only 1 mile. The boss was so disappointed that he asked the blonde, "What went wrong? You were doing just fine."

She told him sadly, "Well, that bucket of paint kept getting farther and farther away."

Bumper Stickers

Your kid may be an honors student, but you're still an idiot.

Learn from your parents' mistakes—use birth control.

I like cats too. Let's exchange recipes.

We have enough youth. How about a Fountain of Smart?

Lottery: A tax on people who are bad at math.

It IS as bad as you think, and they ARE out to get you.

Auntie Em,
Hate you, hate Kansas, taking the dog.
Dorothy.

Time is what keeps everything from happening at once.

Born free...Taxed to death.

Laugh alone, and the world thinks you're an idiot.

Jack Kevorkian for White House Physician.

Montana—At least our cows are sane!

All men are idiots, and I married their king.

If I throw a stick, will you leave?

Sometimes I wake up grumpy—
Other times I let him sleep.

JUST IN CASE HEAVEN IS LIKE THE IRS...
WHEN YOU DO A GOOD DEED, GET A RECEIPT.

SOME PEOPLE ARE ONLY ALIVE BECAUSE IT IS ILLEGAL TO KILL.

A bartender is just a pharmacist with a limited inventory.

I DON'T SUFFER FROM INSANITY, I ENJOY EVERY MINUTE OF IT.

DON'T TELL ME TO "STUFF IT"—I'M A TAXIDERMIST.

OK, who stopped payment on my reality check?

IT'S LONELY AT THE TOP, BUT YOU EAT BETTER.

According to my calculations, the problem doesn't exist.

IRS: WE'VE GOT WHAT IT TAKES TO TAKE WHAT YOU'VE GOT.

REALITY? IS THAT WHERE THE PIZZA DELIVERY GUY COMES FROM?

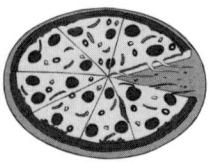

HOW CAN I MISS YOU IF YOU WON'T GO AWAY?

Warning: Dates in calendar are closer than they appear.

GIVE ME AMBIGUITY OR GIVE ME SOMETHING ELSE.

ALWAYS REMEMBER YOU'RE UNIQUE, JUST LIKE EVERYONE ELSE.

Friends help you move. Real friends help you move bodies.

VERY FUNNY, SCOTTY, NOW BEAM DOWN MY CLOTHES.

PURITANISM: THE HAUNTING FEAR THAT SOMEONE, SOMEWHERE MAY BE HAPPY.

Consciousness: That annoying time between naps.

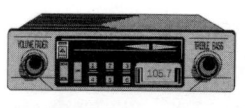

NO RADIO—ALREADY STOLEN.

A day without sunshine is like—well, night.

**Make yourself at home.
Clean my kitchen.**

HONK IF YOU LOVE PEACE AND QUIET.

Just say No! to sex with Pro-lifers.

Taxation WITH representation isn't so hot either!

God is my copilot, but the Devil is my bombardier.

**I don't have a license to kill.
I do have a learner's permit.**

WHO WERE THE BETA-TESTERS FOR
PREPARATIONS A THROUGH G?

Madness takes its toll. Please have exact change.

**If you can read this, I can
hit my brakes and sue you.**

**If you drink, don't park.
Accidents cause people.**

Whitewater is over when the First Lady sings.

**Five days a week my body is a temple. The other
two, it's an amusement park.**

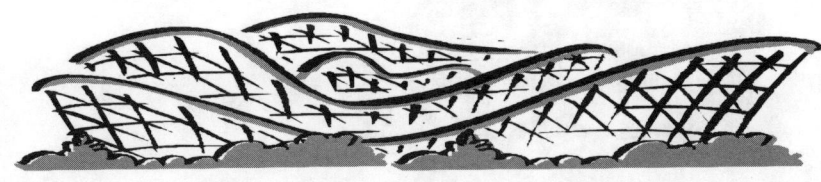

If you take out the killings, Washington actually has a very, very low crime rate!

Former Washington Mayor Marion Barry

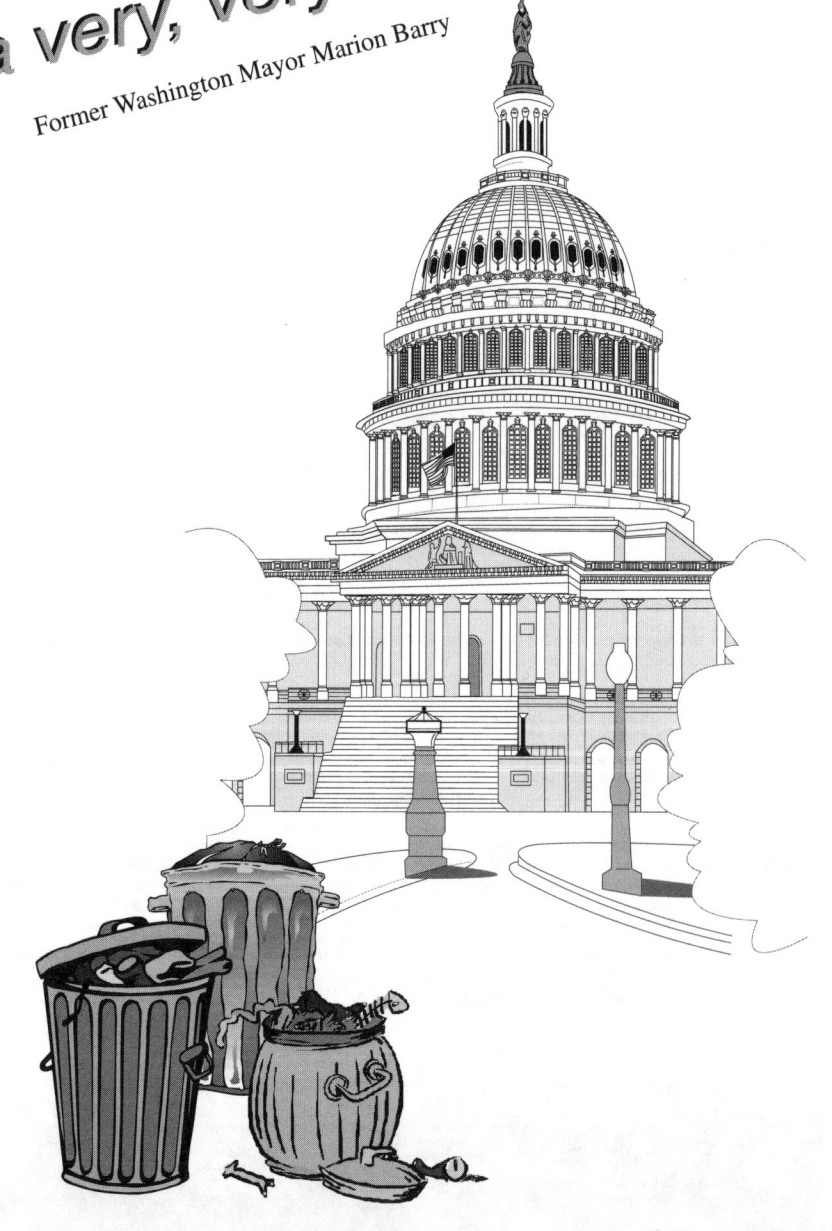

Celebrities

Sometimes the best thing to do is to stop talking, as proved by the following quotes.

Whenever I watch TV and see those poor starving kids all over the world, I can't help but cry. I mean I'd love to be skinny like that, but not with all those flies and death and stuff.
Mariah Carey

Question: If you could live forever, would you, and why?
Answer: I would not live forever, because we should not live forever, because if we were supposed to live forever, then we would live forever, but we cannot live forever, which is why I would not live forever.
Miss Alabama, in the 1994 Miss USA contest

Researchers have discovered that chocolate produces some of the same reactions in the brain as marijuana... The researchers also discovered other similarities between the two but can't remember what they are.
Matt Lauer on NBC's Today Show

I haven't committed a crime. What I did was fail to comply with the law.
New York City Mayor, David Dinkins, on accusations that he failed to pay taxes

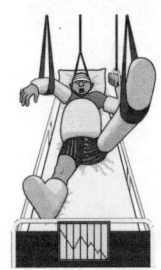

I've never had major knee surgery on any other part of my body.
Winston Bennett, University of Kentucky basketball forward

Traditionally, most of Australia's imports come from overseas.
Former Australian cabinet minister Keppel Enderbery

The police are not here to create disorder.
They are here to preserve disorder.
*Former Chicago Mayor Richard Daley
during 1968 Democratic party Convention*

Without censorship things can get terribly confused in the public mind.
General William Westmoreland during the Vietnam War

China is a big country, inhabited by many Chinese.
Former French President Charles de Gaulle

The streets are safe in Philadelphia. It's only the people who make them unsafe.
Ex-Police Chief and Mayor of Philadelphia

Hmmm...

Have you ever noticed... Anybody going slower than you is an idiot, and anyone going faster than you is a maniac?
George Carlin

You have to stay in shape. My grandmother, she started walking five miles a day when she was 60. She's 97 today, and we don't know where she is.
Ellen DeGeneres

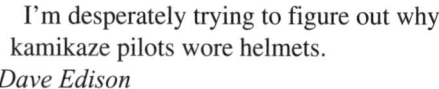

I think men who have a pierced ear are better prepared for marriage. They've experienced pain and bought jewelry.
Rita Rudner

I'm desperately trying to figure out why kamikaze pilots wore helmets.
Dave Edison

Don't spend $2 to dry clean a shirt.
Donate it to the Salvation Army instead.
They'll clean it and put it on a hanger.
Next morning buy it back for 75 cents.
Billiam Coronel

Bigamy is having one wife too many. Monogamy is the same.
Oscar Wilde

I am not a vegetarian because I love animals; I am a vegetarian because I hate plants.
A. Whitney Brown

Half of the people in the world are below average.
Everyone knows this

If a woman has to choose between catching a fly ball and saving an infant's life, she will choose to save the infant's life without even CONSIDERING if there are men on base.
Dave Barry

Somebody hits me, I'm going to hit him back. Even if it does look like he hasn't eaten in a while.
Charles Barkley, after blatantly elbowing an Angolan basketball opponent in the Olympics

If you ever see me getting beaten by the police, put down the video camera and come help me.
Bobcat Goldthwait

Celebrity Viruses...

COLIN POWELL VIRUS
Makes its presence known but doesn't do anything.
Secretly, you wish it would.

HILLARY CLINTON VIRUS
Files disappear, only to reappear mysteriously
a year later in another directory.

O. J. SIMPSON VIRUS
You know it's guilty of trashing your system,
but you can't prove it.

OPRAH WINFREY VIRUS
Your 200MB hard drive suddenly shrinks to 80MB,
and then slowly expands back to 200MB.

PAUL REVERE VIRUS
This revolutionary virus does not horse around. It warns you
of impending hard disk attack: One if by LAN; two if by C:

ADAM AND EVE VIRUS
Takes a couple bytes out of your Apple.

OEDIPUS VIRUS
Your computer becomes obsessed with marrying its own mother board.

RONALD REAGAN VIRUS
Saves your data but forgets where.

MIKE TYSON VIRUS
Quits after one byte.

LORENA BOBBIT VIRUS
Turns your hard disk into a 3½-inch floppy.

ELLEN DeGENERES VIRUS
Your IBM suddenly claims it's a MAC.

SADDAM HUSSEIN VIRUS
Won't let you into any of your programs.

The Traffic Jam...

A guy is driving along the freeway heading for downtown Los Angeles when he finds himself in the middle of a massive traffic jam blocking five freeways. Cars are backed up for miles in all directions.

After a while he notices a guy walking from car to car down the middle of the freeway. He stops at every car to talk to the driver. When the guy reaches him, he rolls down his window and asks, "What's causing all this delay?"

The guy on the freeway says, "You're not going to believe this, but O.J. Simpson is sitting in the middle of the freeway intersection ahead. He's totally distraught. He says there's no way he can ever pay $35 million to the Goldmans and the Browns. So he's threatening to douse himself with gasoline and set himself on fire if people don't give him enough money to cover the judgment. I'm taking up a collection to end this traffic jam."

"How much have you gotten so far?"

"About 10 gallons."

The Things They Say...

Ever wonder if illiterate people get the full effect of alphabet soup?
John Mendoza

Relationships are hard. It's like a full-time job, and we should treat it like one. If your boyfriend or girlfriend wants to leave you, they should give you two-weeks' notice. There should be severance pay, and before they leave you, they should have to find you a temp.
Bob Ettinger

I don't know what's wrong with my television set. I was getting C-Span and the Home Shopping Network on the same station. I actually bought a Congressman.
Bruce Baum

Why does Sea World have a seafood restaurant? I'm halfway through my fishburger when I realize, Oh my God.... I could be eating a slow learner.
Lynda Montgomery

I think war is God's way of teaching us geography.
Paul Rodriguez

I read that love is entirely a matter of chemistry. That must be why my wife treats me like toxic waste.
David Bissonette

When a man steals your wife, there is no better revenge than to let him keep her.
Sacha Guitry

Eighty percent of married men cheat in America. The rest cheat in Europe.
Jackie Mason

Marriage is like a cage; one sees the birds outside desperate to get in and those inside desperate to get out.   *Montaigne*

By all means marry. If you get a good wife, you'll be happy. If you get a bad one, you'll become a philosopher... and that is a good thing for any man.
Socrates

39

New Rules At Reagan Airport...

In keeping with the renaming of National Airport to Ronald Reagan National Airport, the FAA has required the following changes to be made on all flights:

A portion of all ticket sales must be routed to Iran.

No flights will depart between the hours of 1 p.m. to 4 p.m. for "nap time."

Vegetarian meals will consist only of ketchup.

I don't recall.

First-class seating will drastically improve; coach class will be moved to the baggage section.

Should quality concerns arise, baggage handlers are required to invade Dulles to distract critics.

Ticket prices for wealthy passengers will be slashed to increase air travel by the poor.

All passengers are required to shred all travel documents before boarding.

I don't recall.

The pilot's wife must stand behind him in the cockpit so she can tell him what to say to the ground controllers.

"March is one of the most dangerous months to buy stocks. The others are June, January, September, April, November, May, October, July, December, August and February."
Mark Twain

"The first of April is the day we remember what we are the other 364 days of the year."
Mark Twain

Notable Quotes...

Mankind has so far survived all major catastrophes.
It will also survive modern medicine.
Gerhard Kocher

Doctors give medication they know little about, to cure diseases
they know even less about, to people they know nothing about.
Francois de Voltaire

The medical research has made such progress
that there are practically no healthy people anymore.
Aldous Huxley

One is always as happy or unhappy as he thinks.
Kristina of Sweden

Half of modern medicine could be thrown out the window
if one did not feel sorry for the birds.
Martin Henry Fisher

I am dying with the aid of too many doctors.
Alexander the Great

Doctors have throughout time made fortunes on killing their patients with their cures.
The difference in psychiatry is that it is the death of the soul.
R.D. Laving

Anyone who sees a psychiatrist should have his head examined.
Samuel Goldwyn

640KB ought to be enough for anybody.
Bill Gates, 1981

I think there is a world market for maybe five computers.
Thomas Watson, Chairman, IBM, 1943

Words From Women...

I look just like the girls next door...
if you happen to live next door to an amusement park.
Dolly Parton

You see a lot of smart guys with dumb women,
but you hardly ever see a smart woman with a dumb guy.
Erica Jong

Behind every successful man is a surprised woman.
Maryon Pearson

I want to have children, but my friends scare me. One of my friends told me she was in labor for 36 hours. I don't even want to do anything that feels GOOD for 36 hours.
Rita Rudner

I've been on so many blind dates, I should get a free dog.
Wendy Liebman

I found out why cats drink out of the toilet.
My mother told me it's because it's cold in there.
And I'm like: How did my mother know THAT?
Wendy Liebman

I think—therefore I'm single.
Lizz Winstead

When women are depressed, they either eat or go shopping.
Men invade a country.
Elayne Boosler

Our struggle today is not to have a female Einstein get appointed as an assistant professor. It is for a woman schlemiel to get as quickly promoted as a male schlemiel.
Bella Abzug

If high heels were so wonderful,
men would be wearing them.
Sue Grafton

In politics if you want anything said, ask a man;
if you want anything done, ask a woman.
Margaret Thatcher

And...

I have yet to hear a man ask for advice on how to combine marriage and a career.
Gloria Steinem

I never married because there was no need. I have three pets at home, which answer the same purpose as a husband. I have a dog that growls every morning, a parrot that swears all afternoon, and a cat that comes home late at night.
Marie Corelli

If men can run the world, why can't they stop wearing neckties? How intelligent is it to start the day by tying a little noose around your neck?
Linda Ellerbee

I have six locks on my door all in a row. When I go out, I lock every other one. I figure no matter how long somebody stands there picking the locks, they are always locking three.
Elayne Boosler

I'm half-Italian and half-Polish. So I'm always putting a hit out on myself.
Judy Tenuta

Did you ever walk into a room and forget why you walked in? I think that's how dogs spend their lives.
Sue Murphy

The statistics on sanity are that one out of every four Americans is suffering from some form of mental illness. Think of your three best friends. If they're OK, then it's you.
Rita Mae Brown

I ask people why they have a deer's head on their walls. They always say because it's such a beautiful animal. There you go. I think my mother is attractive, but I have photographs of her.
Ellen DeGeneres

Some of us are becoming the men we wanted to marry.
Gloria Steinem

Van Gogh Family Tree...

After much careful research it has been discovered that the artist Vincent Van Gogh had many relatives. Among which were...

His obnoxious brother	Please Gogh
His dizzy aunt	Verti Gogh
The brother who ate prunes	Gotta Gogh
The brother who worked at a convenience store	Stopn Gogh
The grandfather from Yugoslavia	U Gogh
The brother who bleached his clothes white	Hue Gogh
The cousin from Illinois	Chica Gogh
His magician uncle	Wherediddy Gogh
His Mexican cousin	Amee Gogh
The Mexican cousin's American half brother	Grin Gogh
The nephew who drove a stagecoach	Wellsfar Gogh
The constipated uncle	Cant Gogh
The ballroom dancing aunt	Tan Gogh
The bird-lover uncle	Flamin Gogh
His nephew psychoanalyst	E Gogh
The fruit-loving cousin	Man Gogh
An aunt who taught positive thinking	Wayto Gogh
The little nephew	Poe Gogh
A sister who loved disco	Ahgo Gogh
And his niece who travels in a van	Winnie B. Gogh

Ghandi...

Ghandi walked barefoot everywhere, to the point that his feet became thick and hard. Even when he wasn't on a hunger strike, he did not eat much, so he became thin and frail. Due to his meager diet and deteriorating health, he suffered from very bad breath. Nevertheless, he was highly respected as an important spiritual leader.

In other words, he was known as a
super-calloused fragile mystic plagued with halitosis.

Wit of George Carlin...

If it's tourist season, why can't we shoot them?

Since Americans throw rice at weddings,
do Asians throw hamburgers?

Whose cruel idea was it for the word "lisp" to have an "s" in it?

I went for a walk last night and my kids asked me how long I'd be gone. I said, "The whole time."

So what's the speed of dark?

If you're sending someone Styrofoam, what do you pack it in?

I just got skylights put in my place. The people who live above me are furious.

Why do they sterilize needles for lethal injections?

Do they have reserved parking for non-handicapped people at the Special Olympics?

When a man talks dirty to a woman, its sexual harassment. When a woman talks dirty to a man, it's $3.95 per minute.

------------------------------------ if you cut here, you'll probably destroy your monitor.

Smash forehead on keyboard to continue.

Computers & Technology

Silicon Valley Humor...

A man walks into a Silicon Valley pet store to buy a chimpanzee. The store owner points toward three identical chimps in politically correct, animal-friendly natural minihabitats. "The one on the left costs $500," says the store owner.

"Why so much?" asks the customer.

"Because it can program in C," answers the store owner. The customer inquires about the next chimp. "This one costs $1500 because it knows Visual C++ and Object-Relational technology." The startled man then asks about the third chimp. "This one costs $3000," answers the store owner.

"Three thousand dollars!!" exclaims the man. "What can it do?"

"To be honest, I've never seen it do a damn thing," the owner replies, "but it calls itself a consultant."

What If Your Computer Error Messages Appeared In Haiku...

✳✳✳

Three things are certain:
Death, taxes, and lost data.
Guess which has occurred.

✳✳✳

The Web site you seek
Cannot be located but
Endless others exist.

✳✳✳

Chaos reigns within.
Reflect, repent, and reboot.
Order shall return.

✳✳✳

ABORTED effort:
Close all that you have.
You ask way too much.

✳✳✳

First snow, then silence.
This thousand dollar screen dies
so beautifully.

✳✳✳

Windows NT crashed.
I am the Blue Screen of Death.
No one hears your screams.

✳✳✳

With searching comes loss
And the presence of absence:
"My Novel" not found.

✳✳✳

The Tao that is seen
Is not the true Tao, until
You bring fresh toner.

✳✳✳

Serious error.
All shortcuts have disappeared.
Screen. Mind. Both are blank.

✳✳✳

Stay the patient course.
Of little worth is your ire. The
network is down.

✳✳✳

You step in the stream,
But the water has moved on.
This page is not here.

✳✳✳

Rather than a beep
Or a rude error message,
These words: File not found.

✳✳✳

A file that big?
It might be very useful.
But now it is gone.

✳✳✳

A crash reduces
Your expensive computer
to a simple stone.

✳✳✳

Out of memory.
We wish to hold the whole sky,
But we never will.

✳✳✳

Having been erased,
The document you're seeking
Must now be retyped.

✳✳✳

Yesterday it worked
Today it is not working.
Windows is like that.

✳✳✳

An Owed Two The Spelling Checker...

Eye halve a spelling checker
It came with my Pea Sea
It plane lee marks four my revue
Miss steaks aye dew knot sea.

Eye ran this poem threw it,
Your sure reel glad two no.
Its vary polished in it's weigh
My checker tolled me sew.

A checker is a bless sing,
It freeze yew lodes of thyme.
It helps me right awl stiles two reed,
And aides me when aye rime.

Each frays come posed up on my screen
Eye trussed too bee a joule
The checker poured o'er every word
To cheque sum spelling rule.

Be fore a veiling checkers
Hour spelling mite decline,
And if we're lacks oar have a laps,
Wee wood bee maid too wine.

Butt now bee cause my spelling
Is checked with such grate flare,
Their are know faults with in my cite,
Of non eye am a wear.

Now spelling does knot phase me,
It does knot bring a tier.
My pay purrs awl due glad den
With wrapped words fare as hear.

To rite with care is quite a feet
Of witch won should be proud.
And wee mussed dew the best wee can,
Sew flaws are knot aloud.

Sow ewe can sea why aye dew prays
Such soft ware four pea seas,
And why eye brake in two averse
Buy righting won too pleas.

Maxims For The Internet Age...

Home is where you hang your @.

The email of the species is more deadly than the mail.

A journey of a thousand sites begins with a single click.

You can't teach a new mouse old clicks.

Great groups from little icons grow.

Speak softly and carry a cellular phone.

C:\ is the root of all directories.

Don't put all your hypes in one home page.

Pentium wise; pen and paper foolish.

The modem is the message.

Too many clicks spoil the browse.

The geeks shall inherit the earth.

A chat has nine lives.

Fax is stronger than fiction.

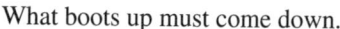

What boots up must come down.

Windows will never cease.

In Gates we trust (and our tender is legal).

Virtual reality is its own reward.

A user and his leisure time are soon parted.

There's no place like http://www.home.com.

Know what to expect before you connect.

Give a man a fish and you feed him for a day;
teach him to use the Net and he won't bother you for weeks.

Little girl to her friend...
"I'm never having kids.
I hear they take nine months to download."

Instructions From The New Information Manager...

Never leave diskettes in the disk drive, as data can leak out of the disk and corrode the inner mechanics of the drive. Diskettes should be rolled up and stored in pencil holders.

Diskettes should be cleaned and waxed once a week. Microscopic metal particles can be removed by waving a powerful magnet over the surface of the disk. Any stubborn metallic shavings can be removed with scouring powder and soap. When waxing diskettes, make sure application is even. This will allow the diskettes to spin faster, resulting in quicker access time.

Do not fold diskettes unless they do not fit into the drive. Fold "big" diskettes in half to use in "little" disk drives.

Never insert a disk into the drive upside down. The data can fall off the surface of the disk, jamming the intricate mechanics of the drive.

Diskettes cannot be backed up by running them through a copier. If you need to back up your data, simply insert two diskettes together into the drive; the data will be updated on both diskettes simultaneously.

Diskettes should not be inserted into or removed from the drive while the light is flashing. Doing so could result in smeared or possibly unreadable text. Occasionally the light continues to flash in what is known as a "hung" or "hooked" state. If your system is "hooking," you will probably need to insert several dollars to gain access to the disk drive.

If your diskette is full and you need more storage space, remove the disk from the drive and shake vigorously for two minutes. This will pack the data ("data compression") enough to allow for more storage. Be sure to cover all the openings with tape to prevent loss of data.

Remember When...

A *computer* was something on TV from a science fiction show
A *window* was something you hated to clean...
And *ram* was a male goat...

Meg was the name of your girlfriend;
and *gig* was your middle finger upright.
Now they all mean different things,
    and that really *megabytes*.

An *application* was used to get a job.
A *program* was a TV show.
A *cursor* was someone using profanity, and a *keyboard* was on a piano.

Memory was something you lost with age.
A *CD* was something you bought to save money.
And if you had a *3½-inch floppy*,
you hoped no one would find out.

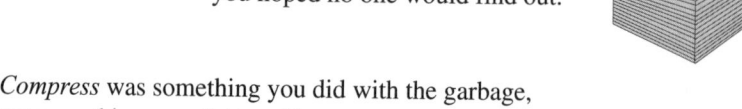

Compress was something you did with the garbage,
not something you did to a file.

And if you *unzipped* anything
in public, you'd lose your job
or go to jail.

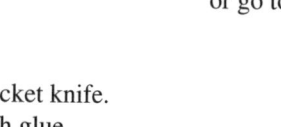

Cut you did with a pocket knife.
Paste you did with glue.
A *web* was a spider's home.
And a *virus* was the flu.

Log-on meant adding wood to a fire.
Hard drive was a long trip by car.
A *mouse pad* was where a mouse lived.
And a *backup* happened to your toilet.

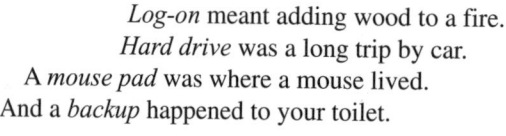

I guess I'll stick to my pad and paper.
And the memory in my head.
I hear nobody's been killed in a computer crash.
But when it happens, they wish they were dead.

Technology For The Country Folk...

Log-On - Making a wood stove hotter

Monitor - Keeping an eye on the wood stove

Download - Gettin the farwood offen the truk

Ram - That thar thing whut splits the farwood

Hard Disk - Gettin home in the wintertime

Prompt - Whut the mail ain't in the wintertime

Windows - Whut to shut when hit's cold outside

Screen - Whut to shut when hit's black fly season

Byte - Whut dem dang flys duz

Chip - Munchie fer the TV

Micro Chip - Whut's in the bottom of the munchie bag

Modem - Whacha did to the hay fields

Dot Matrix - Ole Dan Matrix's wife

Keyboard - Whar ya hang the dang keys

Software - Them dang plastic forks and knifs

Mouse - What eats the grain in the barn

Main Frame - What holds up the barn ruf

Port - Fancy Flatlander wine

Enter - Northerner talk fer C'Mon in y'all

So, What's All This Talk About Microsoft And Cars?

If Microsoft Went Into Automobile Manufacturing...

Every time they repainted the lines on the road, you'd have to buy a new car.

When your car died on the freeway for no reason, you'd accept this, restart, and drive on.

Occasionally, when executing a maneuver caused your car to fail, you'd reinstall the engine. For some strange reason, you'd accept this too.

You could only have one person in the car at a time, unless you had bought "Car95" or "CarNT." But, then you would also have had to buy more seats.

Apple would make a rival car powered by the sun. It would be reliable, five times as fast, twice as easy to drive—but it would only run on five percent of the roads.

Apple car owners could get expensive Microsoft upgrades for their cars, but the upgrades would make their cars run much slower.

You could replace the oil, gas, and alternator warning lights with a single "general car default" warning light.

New seats would force everyone to have the same size butt.

The air bag system would ask "Are you sure?" before deploying.

If you were involved in a crash, you would have no idea what happened.

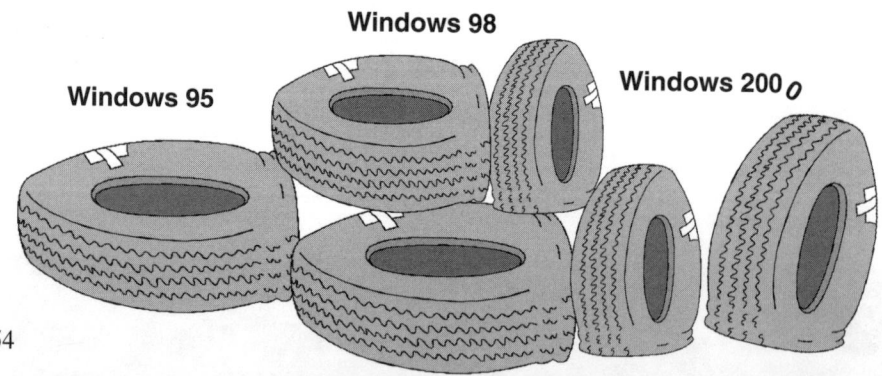

Top Signs Your Coworker Is A Computer Hacker...

You pissed him off last month; this month's phone bill is $20,000.

Massive 401K contribution made in half-cent increments.

He's won the Publisher's Clearing House sweepstakes three years running.

He somehow gets HBO on his PC at work.

His video dating profile lists "public-key encryption" among turn-ons.

For his welcome voice on AOL, you hear, "Good Morning, Mr. President."

You hear him murmur, "Let's see you use that VISA now, Professor 'I-Don't-Give-A's-In-Computer-Science!'"

It's Fixed!!

Boris Yeltsin, Bill Clinton, and Bill Gates were invited to have dinner with God. During dinner He told them: **I need three important people to send my message out to all people—tomorrow I shall destroy the earth.**

Yeltsin immediately called together his cabinet to tell them: "I have two really bad news items for you:
1) God does exist, and
2) Tomorrow He will destroy the earth."

Clinton called an emergency meeting of the Senate and Congress to tell them: "I have good news and bad news:
1) The GOOD news is that God really does exist.
2) The BAD news is, tomorrow He is going to destroy the earth."

Bill Gates went back to Microsoft and very happily announced: "I have two fantastic announcements:
1) I am one of the three most important people on earth.
2) The Y2K problem is solved."

Unknown Computer Viruses...

POLITICALLY CORRECT VIRUS
Never identifies itself as a "virus;" instead refers to itself as an "electronic microorganism."

FEDERAL BUREAUCRAT VIRUS
Divides your hard disk into hundreds of little units, each of which does practically nothing but all of which claim to be the most important part of your computer.

HEALTH CARE VIRUS
Tests your system for a day, finds nothing wrong, and sends you a bill for $4,500.

PROZAC VIRUS
Screws up your RAM, but your processor doesn't care.

JOEY BUTTAFUOCO VIRUS
Only attacks minor files.

SPICE GIRL VIRUS
Has no real function but makes a pretty desktop.

DR. KEVORKIAN VIRUS
Searches your hard drive for old files and deletes them.

AT&T VIRUS
Every three minutes it interrupts you to tell you what great service you're getting.

MCI VIRUS
Every three minutes it reminds you you're paying too much for the AT&T virus.

TEXAS VIRUS
Makes sure it's bigger than any other file.

AIRLINE LUGGAGE VIRUS
You're in Dallas, but your data is in Singapore.

TITANIC VIRUS
Makes your whole computer go down.

DISNEY VIRUS
Everything in the computer goes Goofy.

THEN THERE IS THE CLINTON PC VIRUS
It has a six-inch hard drive and no memory.

Ass Icons...

The little computer symbols we see in emails are called "Emoticons," where ":)" means a smile and ":(" is a frown.

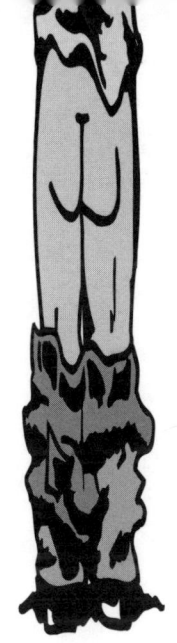

(_!_) a regular ass

(__!__) a fat ass

(!) a tight ass

(_._) a flat ass

(_o_) an ass that's been around

(_O_) an ass that's been around even more

(_X_) leave my ass alone

(_^_) a bubble ass

(_*_) a sore ass

(_!__) a lopsided ass

{_!_} a swishy ass

(_xxx_) kiss my ass

(_zzz_) a tired ass

(_o^o_) a wise ass

(_13_) an unlucky ass

Printed on a sign...
"Salesmen welcome,
dogfood is expensive."

Emerald Dealer

Corporate America

Today's Markets...

Helium is ᵘᵖ, feathers are down.

Paper is stationary.

Fluorescent tubing dims in light trading.

Cows are steering us into a bull market.

Knives are up sharply.

Pencils lose a few points.

Hiking equipment is trailing.

Weights are up in heavy trading.

Elevators are rising, while escalators continue their slow decline.

Light switches are off.

Mining equipment has hit rock bottom.

Diapers remain unchanged.

Shipping lines stay at an even keel.

The market for raisins has dried up.

Coca Cola has fizzled.

Caterpillar stock is inching up.

Sun peaked at midday.

Balloon prices are inflated.

Scott Tissue touches a new bottom.

And batteries explode in an attempt to recharge the market...

Company Slogan BooBoos...

Coors put its slogan, "Turn it loose," into Spanish, where it was read as "Suffer from diarrhea."

Clairol introduced the "Mist Stick," a curling iron, into Germany, only to discover that "mist" is slang for manure. Not too many people had a use for the "manure stick."

Scandinavian vacuum manufacturer Electrolux used the following in an American campaign: "Nothing sucks like an Electrolux."

In Chinese, the Kentucky Fried Chicken slogan, "Finger-Lickin' Good" came out as "Eat your fingers off."

The American slogan for Salem cigarettes, "Salem-Feeling Free," was translated into the Japanese market as "When smoking Salem, you will feel so refreshed that your mind seems to be free and empty."

Colgate introduced a toothpaste in France called "Cue," the name of a porno magazine.

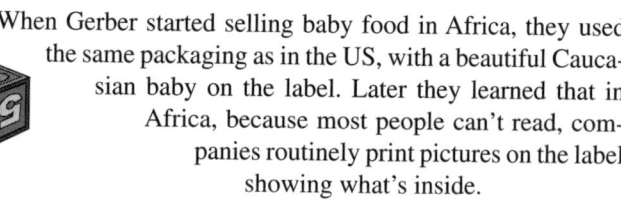

When Gerber started selling baby food in Africa, they used the same packaging as in the US, with a beautiful Caucasian baby on the label. Later they learned that in Africa, because most people can't read, companies routinely print pictures on the label showing what's inside.

An American T-shirt maker in Miami printed shirts for the Spanish market to promote the Pope's visit. Instead of "I saw the Pope" (*El Papá*), the shirts read "I saw the potato" (*la papa*).

"Come alive with the Pepsi Generation" in Chinese translated as "Pepsi brings your ancestors back from the grave."

When Parker Pen marketed a ballpoint pen in Mexico, its ads were supposed to have read "It won't leak in your pocket and embarrass you." Instead, the company thought that the word *"embarazar"* (to impregnate) meant "to embarrass." The unfortunate ad translated as: "It won't leak in your pocket and make you pregnant."

The Coca-Cola name in China was first read as "Ke-kou-ke-la," meaning "Bite the wax tadpole" or "female horse stuffed with wax," depending on the dialect. Coke then researched forty thousand characters to find a phonetic equivalent "ko-kou-ko-le," which translates into "happiness in the mouth."

And finally, not even Nike has been exempt. Nike's television commercial for hiking shoes was shot in Kenya using Samburu tribesmen. The camera closes in on one tribesman who speaks in native Maa. As he speaks, the Nike slogan "Just do it" appears on the screen. An anthropologist at the University of Cincinnati says the Kenyan is really saying, "I don't want these. Give me big shoes." Says Nike's spokeswoman, "We thought nobody in America would know what he said."

Rejected Motel Slogans...

We're working on that smell thing too.
Because you deserve better than the backseat of some car.
As seen on "COPS."
If we'd known you were staying all night, we'd have changed the sheets.
Not just for nooners anymore.
We left off the 9, but you know it's there.
You rented the room, now buy the video.
We'll leave the Lysol for ya!
We don't make adultery. We make adultery better.
It's Hookerriffic!
Blurring the line between stains and avant garde sheet art since 1962!
Cheap and easy—just like your mother.

And the number one rejected motel slogan...

We put the "Ho" in "Hotel."

Actual Instructions Found On Products...

On a string of Chinese-made Christmas lights:
For indoor or outdoor use only.

On Boots children's cough medicine:
Do not drive car or operate heavy machinery.

On a hairdryer:
Do not use while sleeping.

On a hotel shower cap box:
Fits one head.

On packaging for a Rowenta iron:
Do not iron clothes on body.

On Nytol (a sleep aid):
Warning: May cause drowsiness.

On a Japanese food processor:
Not to be used for the other use.

Actual Business Signs...

Outside a radiator repair shop - Best place in town to take a leak.
In a nonsmoking area - If we see you smoking, we will assume you are on fire and take appropriate action.
On maternity room door - Push! Push! Push!
On a front door - Everyone on the premises is a vegetarian except the dog.
At an optometrist's office - If you don't see what you're looking for, you've come to the right place.
On a scientist's door - Gone Fission.
On a taxidermist's window - We really know our stuff.
In a podiatrist's window - Time wounds all heels.
On a butcher's window - Let me meat your needs.
On another butcher's window - Pleased to meat you.
At a used car lot - Secondhand cars in first-crash condition.
At a car dealership - The best way to get back on your feet—miss a car payment.
Outside a muffler shop - No appointment necessary. We'll hear you coming.
Outside a hotel - Help! We need inn-experienced people.
In a dry cleaner's emporium - Drop your pants here.
On a desk in a reception room - We shoot every 3rd salesman; the 2nd one just left.
In a veterinarian's waiting room - Be back in five minutes. Sit! Stay!
At the electric company - We will be delighted if you send in your payment. However, if you don't, you will be.
On a music teacher's door - Out Chopin.
In a beauty shop - Dye now!
In a restaurant window - Don't stand there and be hungry, come in and get fed up.
Inside a bowling alley - Please be quiet. We need to hear a pin drop.
On the door of a computer store - Out for a quick byte.
In front of a funeral home - Drive carefully, we'll wait.
On an electrician's truck - Let us remove your shorts.
On the door of a music library - Bach in a minuet.
In a counselor's office - Growing old is mandatory. Growing wise is optional.

The Bank...

An abrasive young man walks into a bank and says to the teller at the window, "I want to open a damn checking account."

The astonished woman replies, "I beg your pardon, sir. I must have misunderstood you. What did you say?"

"Listen up, damnit. I said I want to open a damn checking account now!"

"I'm very sorry, sir, but that kind of language is not tolerated in this bank."

The teller leaves the window and goes over to the bank manager to inform him of the situation. The manager agrees that the teller does not have to listen to foul language. They both return to the window, and the manager asks the loud customer, "Sir, what seems to be the problem here?"

"There is no damn problem," the man says. "I just won fifty million bucks in the damn lottery and I want to open a damn checking account in this damn bank, OK?"

"I see," says the manager, "and is this bitch giving you a hard time?"

More Good Reasons Why Ad Agencies Should Hire Language Experts...

The Dairy Association's huge success with the campaign "Got Milk?" prompted them to expand advertising to Mexico. It was soon brought to their attention the Spanish translation read "Are you lactating?"

Frank Perdue's chicken slogan "It takes a strong man to make a tender chicken" was translated into Spanish as "It takes an aroused man to make a chicken affectionate."

Big Business At Its Best...

One day while walking down the street a highly successful executive was tragically killed by a bus. St. Peter himself met her soul at the Pearly Gates. "Welcome to Heaven," he said. "Strangely enough, we've never once had an executive make it this far, and we're not really sure what to do with you."

"What we're going to do is let you have a day in Hell and a day in Heaven and then you may decide where you want to spend eternity." "Actually, I think I've made up my mind... I prefer Heaven," said the woman. "Sorry, we have rules. You have to see both."

St. Peter put the executive in an elevator that went down-down-down to Hell. When the doors opened, she found herself stepping onto the putting green of a beautiful golf course with a country club in the distance. Standing in front of her were all her friends—fellow women executives all dressed in evening gowns and cheering for her. They played an excellent round of golf and at night went to the country club, where she enjoyed a perfect steak and lobster dinner. She met the Devil, who was actually rather endearing. She was still having a good time when suddenly it was time to leave. Everybody waved good-bye as she got on the elevator. The elevator went up-up-up and opened back at the Pearly Gates, where St. Peter waited for her. "Now it's time to spend a day in Heaven," he said. So she spent the next 24 hours lounging around on clouds and playing the harp and singing. After 24 hours St. Peter came to her again.

"So, you've spent a day in Hell and a day in Heaven. Now you must choose your eternity," he said. The woman paused for a second and then replied, "Well, I never thought I'd say this. Heaven has been really great and all, but I think I had a better time in Hell."

St. Peter escorted her to the elevator and again she went down-down-down, back to Hell. When the doors of the elevator opened, she found herself standing in a desolate wasteland covered with garbage and filth. She saw her friends dressed in rags, collecting garbage and putting it into sacks. The Devil came up and put his arm around her.

"I don't understand," stammered the woman. "Yesterday there was a golf course and a country club. We ate lobster, danced, and enjoyed ourselves. Now here's a filthy wasteland of garbage, and all my friends look miserable."

The Devil looked at her and smiled. "Yesterday we were recruiting. Today you're staff."

Beauty is in the eye of the beer holder.

Drinking

For The Love Of Guinness...

A professor of chemistry wanted to teach his nineth grade class a lesson about the evils of liquor, so he produced an experiment that involved a glass of water, a pint of Guinness, and two worms.

"Now, class, observe closely the worms," said the professor, as he put a worm into the water. The worm writhed about, happy as a worm in water could be.

He put the second worm into the Guinness. It writhed painfully and quickly sank to the bottom, dead as a doornail. "Now, what lesson can we derive from this experiment?" asked the professor.

A boy sitting in the back answered, "Drink Guinness so you won't get worms."

Irish Joke...

An Irishman had been drinking at a pub all night. The bartender finally told him the bar was closing. So the Irishman stood up to leave and fell flat on his face. He tried to stand again, with the same result. He figured that if he crawled outside, maybe the fresh air would sober him up.

Once outside he stood up again, but then fell flat on his face. So he decided to crawl the four blocks home. When he arrived at his door, he stood up and fell flat on his face again. He crawled through the door and into his bedroom.

When he reached his bed, he tried one more time to stand up. This time he managed to pull himself upright, but he quickly fell right into bed and went sound asleep. He was awakened the next morning by his wife standing over him shouting, "So, you've been out drinking again!!"

"What makes you say that?" he asked, putting on an innocent look.

"The pub called. You left your wheelchair there again."

Harry Had A Bit Of A Drinking Problem...

Every night after dinner Harry took off for the local watering hole. He spent the whole evening there, arriving home around midnight, inebriated.

He always had trouble getting his key into the keyhole to open the door. His wife, waiting up for him, would go to the door and let him in. Then she would proceed to yell and scream at him for going out at night and coming home drunk. But Harry continued his boozy routine.

One day Harry's wife, when she was particularly distraught, was complaining to a friend about her husband's behavior.

After listening to her, the friend said, "Why don't you treat him a little differently when he comes home? Instead of berating him, why don't you give him some loving words and welcome him home with a kiss? Then he might change his ways."

The wife thought the idea was worth trying.

That night after dinner Harry took off again. And about midnight he arrived home in his usual condition. When his wife heard him struggling with his keys, she quickly opened the door and let Harry inside.

This time instead of berating him as she had done before, she took his arm and led him into the living room. She sat him down in an easy chair, put his feet up on the ottoman, and took off his shoes. Then she went behind him and started to cuddle him. After a while she said to him, "It's pretty late. I think we had better go upstairs to bed now, don't you?"

At that, Harry replied, in his inebriated state, "I guess we might as well. I'll get in trouble when I get home anyway!"

Set 'em Up While I Put You Down...

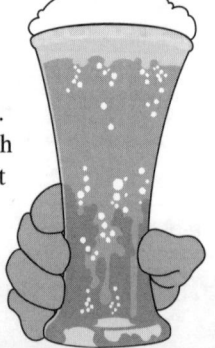

One day Mr. Coors, Mr. Busch, and Mr. Guinness (the beer magnates) met for lunch. Coors ordered a Coors beer to drink, and Busch ordered a Budweiser. Guinness ordered a Diet Coke. The others asked him why he had ordered a Coke. He replied, "As long as you guys aren't drinking beer, I'm won't either."

The Saxophone...

The morning after a night on the town Bob told his friend Tom about the Golden Club where he had been drinking. Everything in the club was lined with gold. The glasses had a gold rim, the rail on the bar was plated with gold, even the urinals were gold-plated.

Tom was ready to believe his buddy until he mentioned the gold-plated urinals. So he phoned the Golden Club. "Is it true that the glasses in your club have a gold rim?" Tom asked.

"Yes, it's true" replied the voice on the other end.

"And is the rail on the bar plated with gold?" asked Tom.

"Yes, it is" was the reply from the other end.

"And, one more thing, is it true that the urinals are gold-plated?" inquired Tom.

Tom could hear the person on the other end yell to the band, "Hey, Joe, I think I found the guy from last night who peed in your saxophone!"

Say, That Sounds Logical...

A herd of buffalo can only move as fast as the slowest buffalo. When the herd is hunted, the slowest and weakest ones at the back that are killed first. This natural selection is good for the herd as a whole, because the general speed and health of the whole keeps improving by the regular culling of the weakest members. In much the same way, the human brain can operate only as fast as the slowest brain cells. Excessive intake of alcohol, we all know, kills off brain cells, but naturally it attacks the slowest and weakest brain cells first. In this way, regular consumption of beer eliminates the weaker cells, constantly making the brain a faster, more efficient machine.

The Decoy...

One night a police officer was staking out a particularly rowdy bar for possible violations of driving-under-the-influence laws. At closing time he saw a fellow stumble out of the bar, trip on the curb, and try his keys on five different cars before he found his. Then he sat fumbling around with his keys for several minutes while everyone else left the bar and drove off. Finally the man started his engine and pulled away. The police officer was waiting. He stopped the driver, read him his rights, and administered the breathalyzer test. The results showed a reading of 0.0. The puzzled officer demanded to know how this could be. The driver replied,

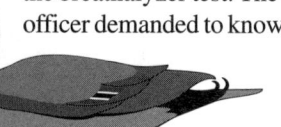

"Simple. Tonight I'm the designated decoy."

What A Way To Go...

Brenda O'Malley was home making dinner as usual when Tim Finnegan arrived at her door. "Brenda, may I come in?" he asked. "I've somethin' to tell ya."

"Of course you may. You're always welcome, Tim. But where's my husband?"

"That's what I'm here to be tellin' ya, Brenda. There was an accident down at the Guinness brewery..."

"Oh, God no!" cries Brenda. "Please don't tell me..."

"I must, Brenda. I'm sorry. Your husband Shamus is dead and gone."

Brenda reached a hand out to her side, found the arm of the rocking chair by the fireplace, pulled the chair to her, and collapsed into it. She wept for many minutes. Finally she looked up at Tim. "How did it happen, Tim?"

"It was terrible, Brenda. He fell into a vat of Guinness Stout and drowned."

"Oh, my dear Jesus! But you must tell me true, Tim. Did he at least go quickly?"

"Well, no Brenda......not exactly."

"No?"

"Fact is, he got out three times to pee."

Two Vampires...

Two vampires walked into a bar and called for the bartender.

"I'll have a glass of blood," said one. "I'll have a glass of plasma," said the other.

"OK," replied the bartender, "that'll be one blood and one blood lite."

My designated driver drove me to drink.

I'M NOT AS THINK AS YOU DRUNK I AM.

I am filthy, stinking rich.
Well, two out of three ain't bad.

The Thief...

An Irishman walks out of a pub, stumbling back and forth with a key in his hand. A cop on the beat sees him and approaches, "Can I help you, lad?"

"Yesss, ssshombody shtole me car!" the Irishman replies.

The cop asks, "Well now, where was your car the last time you saw it?"

"It was at the end of this key." About this time the cop looks down to see the Irishman's member hanging out for all to see.

He then asks, "Are you aware that you're exposing yourself?"

The Irishman looks down woefully and moans, "OOH GOD...they got me girlfriend too!"

Kid With An Attitude...

"Gimme a double whiskey!" the little boy yelled to the barmaid on entering the saloon.
"Do you want to get me in trouble?" she asked.
The kid replied, "Maybe later. Right now I just want a drink."

Being A Man Is Hard Work...

An irate wife was complaining about her husband spending all his time at the pub, so one night he took her along with him.

"What'll ya have?" he asked.

"Oh, I don't know. The same as you I suppose," she replied.

So the husband ordered a couple of Jack Daniel's and threw his "down the hatch" in one go. His wife watched him, then took a sip from her glass, and immediately spat it out.

"Yuck, it's Bloody AWFUL!!!" she spluttered. "I don't know how you can drink this stuff!"

"Well, there you go," cried the husband. "And YOU think I'm out enjoying myself every night!"

An All-Nighter...

At 3 a.m. a desk clerk at a hotel gets a call from a drunk asking what time the bar opens. "It opens at noon," answers the clerk.

About an hour later he gets a call from the same guy, sounding even drunker. "What time does the bar open?" he asks.

"Same time as before... noon." replies the clerk.

Another hour passes and he calls again, plastered. "Whatjooshay the bar opins at?"

The clerk then answers, "It opens at noon, but if you can't wait, I can have room service send something up to you."

"No... I don't wanna git **in**... Ah wanna git **out**!"

Drinking Guide For The Holidays...

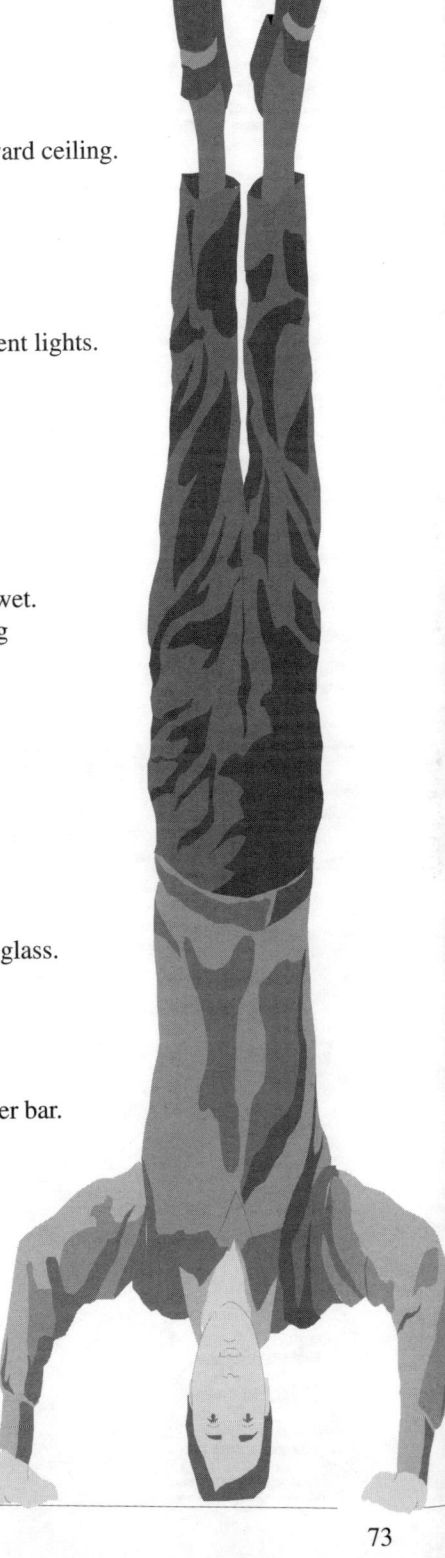

Symptom - Feet cold and wet.
Fault - Glass being held at incorrect angle.
Action - Rotate glass so that open end points toward ceiling.

Symptom - Beer unusually pale and tasteless.
Fault - Glass empty.
Action - Get someone to buy you another beer.

Symptom - Opposite wall covered with fluorescent lights.
Fault - You have fallen over backward.
Action - Have yourself lashed to bar.

Symptom - Mouth contains cigarette butts.
Fault - You have fallen forward.
Action - See above.

Symptom - Beer tasteless, front of your shirt is wet.
Fault - Mouth not open or glass applied to wrong part of face.
Action - Retire to restroom, practice in mirror.

Symptom - Feet warm and wet.
Fault - Improper bladder control.
Action - Stand next to nearest dog, complain about her housebreaking.

Symptom - Floor blurred.
Fault - You're looking through bottom of empty glass.
Action - Get someone to buy you another beer.

Symptom - Floor moving.
Fault - You're being carried out.
Action - Find out if you are being taken to another bar.

Symptom - Room seems unusually dark.
Fault - Bar has closed.
Action - Confirm home address with bartender.

Symptom - Taxi suddenly takes on colorful aspect and textures.
Fault - Beer consumption has exceeded personal limitations.
Action - Cover mouth.

To steal ideas from one person is plagiarism; to steal from many is research.

Education

Check Those Nails...

A 10-year-old Jewish boy was failing math. His parents tried everything from tutors to hypnosis, to no avail.

Finally, at the insistence of a family friend, they decided to enroll their son in a private Catholic school.

After the first day the boy's parents were surprised when he walked in after school with a stern, focused, very determined expression on his face. Obviously something had happened.

He went straight past them right to his room, and quietly closed the door. For nearly two hours he toiled away—with math books strewn about his desk and on the surrounding floor. He emerged long enough to eat, and after quickly cleaning his plate, he went straight back to his room, closed the door, and studied feverishly until bedtime.

This pattern of behavior continued until it was time for the first quarter's report card. The boy walked in with it unopened, laid it on the dinner table, and went straight to his room. Cautiously his mother opened it and, to her amazement, under "Math" she saw a large red "A."

Overjoyed, she and her husband rushed into their son's room, thrilled at his remarkable progress.

"Was it the nuns that did it?" the father asked.

The boy shook his head "No."

"Was it the one-on-one tutoring? Or the peer-mentoring?" "No."

"The textbooks? The teachers? The curriculum?" "No," said the son.

"The first day when I walked in the front door, I saw that guy nailed to the plus sign. I KNEW they meant business!"

Hell...

A thermodynamics professor had written a take-home exam for his graduate students. It had but one question: Is Hell exothermic or endothermic? Support your answer with adequate proof.

Most of the students wrote proof of their beliefs using Boyle's Law or some variant. One student, however, wrote the following:

First, we postulate that if souls exist, then they must have some mass. If they do, then a mole of soles can also have mass. So, at what rate are souls moving into Hell and at what rate are souls leaving? I think we can safely assume that once a soul gets to Hell, it will not leave. Therefore, no souls are leaving Hell. As for the souls entering Hell, lets look at the different religions that exist in the world today. Some of these religions state that if you are not a member of their religion, you will go to Hell. Because there is more than one of these religions and people normally do not belong to more than one religion, we can project that all people and all souls go to Hell. With birth and death rates as they are, we can expect the number of souls in Hell to increase exponentially. Now, we look at the rate of change in volume in Hell. Boyle's Law states that in order for the temperature and pressure in Hell to stay the same, the ratio of the mass of souls to volume must remain constant.

#1: So, if Hell is expanding at a slower rate than the rate at which souls enter Hell, then the temperature and pressure in hell will increase until all Hell breaks loose.

#2: Of course, if Hell is expanding at a rate faster than the increase of souls in Hell, then the temperature and pressure will drop until Hell freezes over.

So which is it? If we accept the postulate given to me by Theresa Banyan during freshman year, "It will be a cold night in Hell before I sleep with you," and take into account the fact that I have not succeeded in having sexual relations with her, then #2 cannot be true. Therefore, Hell is exothermic.

The student received the only A.

Ooopps...

One day a young female teacher was giving an assignment to her sixth grade class. It was a large assignment, so she started writing high up on the chalkboard. Suddenly there was a giggle from one of the boys in the class. She quickly turned and asked, "What's so funny, Pat?"

"Well, Teacher, I just saw your garter."

"Get out of my classroom," she ordered, "And stay out for three days."

The teacher turned back to the chalkboard. Realizing she had forgotten to title the assignment, she reached to the very top of the board. Suddenly there was an even louder giggle from another male student. She wheeled around, "What's so funny, Billy?"

"Well, Ma'am, I just saw both your garters."

She commanded, "Get out of my classroom!" This time the punishment was more severe, "I don't want to see you for three weeks."

Embarrassed and frustrated, she dropped the eraser when she turned around. As she bent over to pick it up, there was a burst of laughter from another male student. She quickly turned to see Little Johnny dashing out of the classroom.

"Where do you think you are going?" she asked.

"Well, Teacher, with what I just saw, my school days are over."

College Rules...

On the first day of college the dean addressed the students to point out some of the rules:

"The female dormitory is out-of-bounds for all male students, and the male dormitory to the female students. Anybody caught breaking this rule will be fined $20 the first time. Anybody caught breaking this rule the second time will be fined $60. Being caught a third time will incur a hefty fine of $180. Are there any questions?"

At this point a male student in the crowd inquired, "How much for a season pass?"

You Must Be A Teacher If...

You believe the staff room should have a Valium salt lick.

You find humor in other people's stupidity.

You want to slap the next person who says, "Must be nice to have all your holidays and summers free."

You can tell it's a full moon without ever looking outside.

You believe "shallow gene pool" should have it's own box on the report card.

You believe that unspeakable evil will befall you if anyone says, "Boy, the kids are sure mellow today."

When out in public, you feel the urge to talk to strange children and correct their behavior.

Giving all A's on the report card would make your life SOOO much simpler.

When you mention "vegetables" and you're not talking about a food group.

You think people should be required to get a government permit before being allowed to reproduce.

You wonder how some parents ever MANAGED to reproduce.

You believe in aerial spraying of Prozac.

You really encourage an obnoxious parent to check into home schooling.

Meeting a child's parents INSTANTLY answers the question "Why is this kid like this?"

I HAVE A DEGREE IN LIBERAL ARTS... DO YOU WANT FRIES WITH THAT?

You who think you know it all are damned annoying to those of us who do.

I believe five out of four people have trouble with fractions.

Double Positive...

A linguistics professor was lecturing to his class one day. "In English," he said, "a double negative forms a positive. In some languages though, such as Russian and Spanish, a double negative is still a negative.

However, there is no language wherein a double positive forms a negative."

A voice in the back of the room piped up,

"Yeah, Right."

Farmyard Johnnie...

A primary school teacher decided to expand the horizons of her students. During the visit to a nearby farm, she challenged the children to raise their hands if they knew the correct sound made by each animal.

"Who knows what sound a cow makes?" she asked.

Cindie willingly and politely raised her hand and said, "Moooo!"

"Very good, Cindie," replied the teacher, "and what sound do sheep make?"

"Baaaa," answered Jimmy. She continued this for a while. Then she asked, "And what sound does a pig make?"

All the children in the class raised their hands at once! She was surprised at the response.

"Lil' Johnnie, go ahead and tell us the sound the pig makes," she encouraged.

He composed himself, took a deep breath and bellowed, "Up against the wall and spread 'em, you little thief!"

So, an Arab, a Catholic, and a Jew go into this bar...

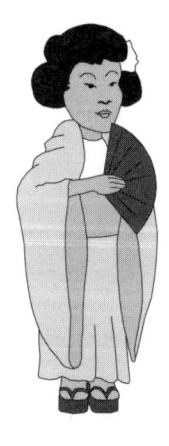

Ethnic Jokes

The Eskimo...

An Eskimo takes his snowmobile in for service. The mechanic checks it out and says to the Eskimo, "It looks like you've blown a seal."

"No," says the Eskimo, "that's just frost on my moustache."

After years of expensive and dangerous work at the site of the *Titanic* sinking, Irish salvage today raised the iceberg.

The Indians...

An Indian brave named Sitting Bull comes home to the wigwam and informs his father that he's found a wonderful new Jewish girlfriend and they're getting married. Naturally the father is upset. "Why don't you find a nice Indian girl? It's not right for Indians to marry out. Anyway, I'm sure that Jews feel the same way. Surely they're not thrilled with having an Indian son-in-law."

"Not true!" replies the brave. "They like me so much that they've already given their daughter a new Indian name."

"What's that?" asks the father.

"Sitting Shiva."

Explanatory note: When a Jewish person passes away, his or her closest living relative observes a death ritual for seven days. This is called "Sitting Shiva." I know, I know, if you have to explain a joke, it takes away from the humor. But sometimes it's necessary.

The True Meanings Of Asian Names...

Wa Shing Kah	Cleaning an automobile
Wai So Dim	Are you trying to save electricity?
Wai U Shao Ting	There is no reason to raise your voice.
Ai Bang Mai Ne	I bumped into the coffee table.
Chin Tu Fat	You need a face lift.
Dung On Mai Shu	I stepped in #$%*.
Dum Gai	A stupid person
Gun Pao Der	An ancient Chinese invention
Hu Flung Dung	Which one of you fertilized the field?
Hu Yu Hai Ding	We have reason to believe you are harboring a fugitive.
Jan Ne Ka Sun	A former late night talk show host
Kum Hia	Approach me.
Lao Ze Sho	Gilligan's Island
Lao Zi	Not very good
Lin Ching	An illegal execution
Moon Lan Ding	A great achievement of the American space program
Ne Ahn	A lighting fixture used in advertising signs
Shai Gai	A bashful person
Tai Ne Bae Be	A premature infant
Tai Ne Po Ne	A small horse
Tai Ne Ba Bol	A Don Ho song (see "Yu Mai Te Tan," below)
Ten Ding Ba	Serving drinks to people
Wan Bum Lung	A person with TB or Cancer
Yu Mai Te Tan	Your vacation in Hawaii agrees with you

Nothing Changes...

Sometime in the 1970s a shipment of meat arrives in a village in the Soviet Union. The townspeople line up at the store to receive their rations. After about an hour an official comes out of the store to announce, "Comrades, I'm sorry to tell you, but there isn't enough meat for everyone, so the Jews have to leave." Grumbling, the Jews leave.

About an hour later the official comes out of the store to announce, "Comrades, I'm sorry to tell you, but there isn't enough meat for everyone, so anyone who is not a member of the Communist party will have to leave." More grumbling as the non-Party members depart.

Another hour goes by and the official comes out of the store again to announce, "Comrades, I'm sorry to tell you, but there isn't enough meat for everyone in the line, so anyone who wasn't a member of the Party before 1956 has to leave." More grumbling as all the younger Party members leave. A few old people remain in the line.

Yet another hour passes. By now it has grown dark and cold. The same official comes out of the store to announce, "Comrades, I'm sorry to tell you this, but there isn't any meat. Go home."

One old lady in the line turns to her neighbor and says, "See? It's like I told you. The Jews always get the best treatment!"

A Polish And Italian Story...

An Italian is walking down the street when he sees a Polak with a very long pipe and a yardstick. He's standing the pipe on its end and trying to reach the top of it with his yardstick. Seeing the Polak's ignorance, the Italian wrenches the pipe out of his hand, lays it on the sidewalk, measures it with the yardstick, and says,

"There, 11 feet long!"

The Polak grabs the yardstick and shouts, "You idiot Italian! I don't care how long it is! I want to know how high it is!"

Some Modern Things Are Good...

An Amish boy and his father were visiting a mall. They were amazed by almost everything they saw, especially by two shiny silver walls that moved apart and back together again. The boy asked his father,

"What is this, Father?"

The father, never having seen an elevator, responded, "Son I have never seen anything like this in my life. I don't know what it is."

While the boy and his father were watching wide-eyed, an old lady in a wheel chair rolled up to the moving walls and pressed a button. The walls opened, and the lady rolled between them into a small room, and then the shiny walls closed. The boy and his father watched as small numbered lights lit up above the walls. Then they watched as the numbers lit up in the reverse direction. The walls opened again, and a beautiful 24-year-old woman stepped out.

The father said to his son, "Go get your mother."

Polish Joke #1263...

A small two-seater Cessna plane crashed in a cemetery early this afternoon in central Poland. Polish search and rescue workers have recovered three hundred bodies so far and expect that number to climb as digging continues into the evening.

Say What...

A Jewish boy comes home from school and tells his mother he has been given a part in the school play.

"Wonderful," says the mother, "What part is it?"

The boy says, "I play the part of the Jewish husband!"

The mother scowls and says, "Go back and tell your teacher you want a speaking part."

The Jewish Parrot...

A Jewish widower bought a parrot for companionship. The two of them talked and talked, and the man began teaching the bird Yiddish. He told the parrot about his father's coming to America, about his mother as a young bride, about his family.

In the morning the man began his prayers. The parrot demanded to know what he was doing, and when the widower explained, the parrot wanted to pray too. The man had a miniature *yamulke* made for the bird. The parrot wanted to learn to read Hebrew, so the man spent months teaching it to read the Torah. In time the man came to love the parrot as a friend and as a Jew. He was lonely no more.

On Rosh Hashanah the man rose and got dressed. He was about to leave for the synagogue when the parrot demanded to go with him. The man explained that was no place for a bird, but the parrot made a terrific argument and so rode to the synagogue on the man's shoulder.

Needless to say, the pair made quite a spectacle, and the man was questioned by everyone, including the Rabbi. At first, the Rabbi refused to allow a bird into the building on High Holy Days, but the man persuaded him to let him in this one time, swearing that the parrot could also pray in Hebrew.

Suddenly wagers were made with the man. Thousands of dollars were bet that the parrot could not speak Yiddish or Hebrew, much less pray in a second language. Some bettors even offered odds.

During services all eyes were on the parrot. It perched on the man's shoulder as one prayer and song passed. There was not a peep from the bird. The man became annoyed, slapping at his shoulder and mumbling under his breath, "Pray already!" But the parrot said nothing. "Pray...parrot, you can pray, so pray, come on, everybody's looking at you!" The parrot said nothing.

After Rosh Hashanah services were concluded, the man found he owed his synagogue buddies (and the Rabbi) more than $4,000 dollars. He marched home, saying nothing. Finally, several blocks from the temple, the bird began to sing an old Yiddish song as happy as a lark.

The man stopped and stared at him. "You miserable bird, you cost me over $4,000 dollars today. Why? I taught you morning prayers, taught you to read Hebrew and the Torah. You begged me to bring you to a synagogue on Rosh Hashanah, why? Why did you do this to me?"

"Don't be a schmuck," the parrot replied. "Think of the odds on Yom Kippur!"

Save the whales:
Collect the
whole set.

Government

My Dog's Better Than Your Dog...

Four men were bragging about how smart their dogs were. The first man was an engineer, the second man an accountant, the third man a chemist, and the fourth a government worker.

To show off, the engineer called to his dog, "T-Square, do your stuff." T-Square trotted over to a desk, took out paper and a pen, and promptly drew a circle, a square, and a triangle. Everyone agreed that was good.

The accountant said his dog could do better. He called to his dog and said, "Slide Rule, do your stuff." Slide Rule went to the kitchen and returned with a dozen cookies. He divided them into four equal piles of three cookies each. Everyone agreed that was clever.

But the chemist said his dog could do better. He called to his dog and said, "Measure, do your stuff." Measure got up, walked over to the fridge, took out a quart of milk, got a 10-ounce glass from the cupboard, and poured exactly eight ounces without spilling a drop. Everyone agreed that was smart.

The three men turned to the government worker and said, "What can your dog do?" The government worker called to his dog and said, "Coffee Break, do your stuff."
Coffee Break jumped to his feet, ate the cookies, drank the milk, dumped on the paper, sexually assaulted the other three dogs, claimed he injured his back while doing so, filed a grievance for unsafe working conditions, put in for worker's compensation, then went home on sick leave.

Necessity Breeds Ingenuity...

During the heat of the space race in the 1960s the U.S. National Aeronautics and Space Administration decided it needed a ballpoint pen to write in the zero-gravity confines of its space capsules.

After considerable research the Astronaut Pen was developed at a cost of about US$1 million. It worked in space, and it also enjoyed a modest success as a novelty item back here on earth.

The Soviet Union, faced with the same problem, used a pencil.

David And Goliath...

This is the transcript of a radio conversation between a U.S. naval ship and Canadian authorities off the coast of Newfoundland.

Canadians: Please divert your course 15 degrees south to avoid a collision.
Americans: Recommend you divert your course 15 degrees north to avoid a collision.
Canadians: Negative. You will have to divert your course 15 degrees south to avoid a collision.
Americans: This is the Captain of a U.S. Navy ship. I say again, divert YOUR course.
Canadians: No. I say again, you divert YOUR course.
Americans: THIS IS THE AIRCRAFT CARRIER USS LINCOLN, THE SECOND LARGEST SHIP IN THE UNITED STATES ATLANTIC FLEET. WE ARE ACCOMPANIED BY THREE DESTROYERS, THREE CRUISERS, AND NUMEROUS SUPPORT VESSELS. I DEMAND THAT YOU CHANGE YOUR COURSE 15 DEGREES NORTH, I SAY AGAIN, THAT'S ONE FIVE DEGREES NORTH, OR COUNTERMEASURES WILL BE UNDERTAKEN TO ENSURE THE SAFETY OF THIS SHIP.
Canadians: This is a lighthouse. Your call.

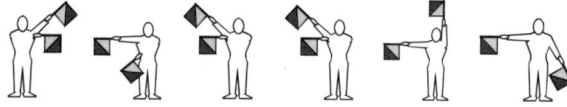

We're From The Government, And We're Your Friends...

A young woman from California purchased a piece of timberland in Oregon. There was a large tree on one of the highest points on the tract. She wanted to get a good view of her land, so she started to climb the big tree. As she neared the top, she encountered a spotted owl, which attacked her.

In her haste to escape, she slid down the tree to the ground, getting many splinters in her private parts. In considerable pain she hurried to the nearest doctor.

He listened to her story, then told her to go into the examining room where he would see if he could help her. She sat waiting for three hours before the doctor reappeared.

The angry woman demanded, "What took you so long?" He replied, "I had to get permits from the Environmental Protection Agency, the Forest Service, and the Bureau of Land Management before I could remove old-growth timber from a recreational area."

Dress Code...

A man who was called for an audit at the IRS asked his accountant what to wear.

"Wear your shabbiest clothing. Let them think you are a pauper," the accountant replied.

When he asked his lawyer the same question, he got the opposite advice. "Don't let them intimidate you. Wear your most elegant suit and tie."

Confused, the man went to his Rabbi, told him of the conflicting advice, and requested a resolution of his dilemma.

"Let me tell you a story," replied the Rabbi. "A bride asked her mother what to wear on her wedding night. 'Wear a long heavy flannel nightgown that goes right up to your neck.' But when she asked her best friend, she got conflicting advice. 'Wear your sexiest negligee with a V-neck right down to your navel.'"

The man protested, "What does a bride have to do with my problem with the IRS?"

"No matter what you wear, you are going to get screwed."

Service Charge...

A little boy needed $100 very badly, so his mother told him to pray to God for it. He prayed and prayed for two weeks, but nothing turned up. So he decided to write God a letter requesting the money. When the postal authorities received the letter addressed to God, they opened it and decided to send it to the President. The President was so impressed, touched, and amused that he instructed his secretary to send the little boy $5. He thought $5 would be a lot of money to the little boy. The little boy was delighted with the $5 and sat down to write a thank-you letter to God, which read as follows:

Dear God,
Thank you very much for sending the money. I noticed that You had to send it through Washington. As usual, those morons deducted $95. Thanks anyway!

A penny saved is a Congressional oversight.

Or Blood From A Turnip...

The local bar was so sure that its bartender was the strongest man around that they offered a standing $1000 bet.

The bartender would squeeze a lemon until all the juice ran into a glass and hand the lemon to a patron. Anyone who could squeeze one more drop of juice out would win the money.

Many people had tried over time (weightlifters, longshoremen, etc.)—but nobody could do it.

One day a scrawny little man came in, wearing thick glasses and a polyester suit, and said in a tiny, squeaky voice, "I'd like to try the bet."

After the laughter had died down, the bartender said OK, grabbed a lemon, and squeezed. He then handed the wrinkled remains of the rind to the little man.

But the crowd's laughter turned to silence as the man clenched his fist around the lemon and six drops fell into the glass.

As the crowd cheered, the bartender paid the $1000, and asked the little man, "What do you do for a living? Are you a lumberjack or a weightlifter, or what?"

The man replied, "I work for the IRS."

Don't Steal.
The government hates competition.

The trouble with political jokes is they get elected.

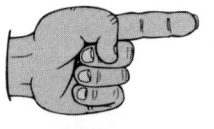
"Suppose you were an idiot.
Suppose you were a Congressman.
But I repeat myself."
Mark Twain
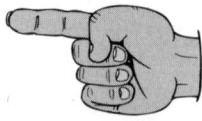

What State Mottos Should Be...

Alabama:
At Least We're Not Mississippi

Arkansas:
Litterasy Ain't Everthing

California:
As Seen On TV

Georgia:
We Put The "Fun" In Fundamentalist Extremism

Idaho:
More Than Just Potatoes... Well, OK, We're Not, But The Potatoes Sure Are Real Good

Illinois:
Gateway To Iowa

Indiana:
Two Billion Years Tidal Wave Free

Kansas:
First Of The Rectangle States

Kentucky:
Five Million People; Fifteen Last Names

Louisiana:
We're Not All Drunk Cajun Wackos, That's Just Our Tourism Campaign

Maryland:
A Thinking Man's Delaware

Michigan:
First Line Of Defense From Canadians

Minnesota:
For Sale

Mississippi:
Come Feel Better About Your Own State

Montana:
Land Of The Big Sky, The Unibomber, And Very Little Else

Nebraska:
Ask About Our State Motto Contest

Nevada:
Whores And Poker!

New Hampshire:
Go Away and Leave Us Alone

New Jersey:
You Want A ##$%##! Motto? I Got Yer ##$%##! Motto Right Here!

New York:
You Have The Right To Remain Silent, You Have The Right To An Attorney

North Carolina:
Tobacco Is A Vegetable

North Dakota:
Um... We've Got... Um... Dinosaur Bones? Yeah, Dinosaur Bones!

Oregon:
Spotted Owl, It's What's For Dinner

Texas:
¿Se habla inglés?

Utah:
Our Jesus Is Better Than Your Jesus

West Virginia:
One Big Happy Family—Really!

Take my wife... Please!

Henny Youngman
A Tribute

The all-time king of the one-liner recently died at 91. Henny Youngman had enjoyed a long wonderful career in comedy. His most memorable line "Take my wife, please," is a classic of half a century. In loving memory of the master...

Getting on a plane, I told the ticket lady, "Send one of my bags to New York, send one to Los Angeles, and send one to Miami." She said, "We can't do that!" I told her, "You did it last week!"

The Doctor says, "You'll live to be 60!"
"I AM 60!"
"See, what did I tell you?"

A doctor says to a man, "You want to improve your love life? You need to get some exercise. Run 10 miles a day." Two weeks later, the man calls the doctor. The doctor asks, "How is your love life since you've been running?" "I don't know, I'm 140 miles away!"

The doctor says to the patient, "Take your clothes off and stick your tongue out the window." "What will that do," asks the patient. The doctor says, "I'm mad at my neighbor!"

Doctor says to a man, "You're pregnant!" The man says, "How does a man get pregnant?" The doctor says, "The usual way, a little wine, a little dinner...."

A man says to a psychiatrist, "Nobody listens to me!"
The doctor says, "Next!"

I had a nightmare last night.
I dreamed Dolly Parton was my mother
and I was a bottle baby.

Someone stole all my credit cards, but I won't be reporting it. The thief spends less than my wife did.

A bum asked me, "Give me $10 till payday." I asked, "When's payday?" He said, "I don't know, you're the one who's working!"

The horse I bet on was so slow the jockey kept a diary of the trip.

My horse's jockey was hitting the horse. The horse turns around and says, "Why are you hitting me, there's nobody behind us!"

A bum came up to me saying, "I haven't eaten in two days!" I said, "You should force yourself!"

She's been married so many times she has rice marks on her face.

"What's the latest dope on Wall Street?" "My son!"

Why do Jewish divorces cost so much? They're worth it.

Why do Jewish men die before their wives? They want to.

Why don't Jews drink? It interferes with their suffering.

A car hit a Jewish man. The paramedic says, "Are you comfortable?" The man says, "I make a good living."

If my mother knew I did this for a living, she'd kill me. She thinks I'm selling dope.

Now, The Longer Jokes...

A priest is sent to Alaska. A bishop goes up to visit one year later. The bishop asks, "How do you like it up here?"

The priest says, "If it weren't for my Rosary, and two martinis a day, I'd be lost. Bishop, would you like a martini?"

"Yes."

"Rosary, get the bishop a martini!"

A honeymoon couple is in the Watergate Hotel in Washington. The bride is concerned "What if the place is still bugged?" The groom says, "I'll look for a bug." He looks behind the drapes, behind the pictures, under the rug. "AHA!" Under the rug was a disc with four screws. He gets his Swiss Army knife, unscrews the screws and throws them and the disc out the window. The next morning, the hotel manager asks the newlyweds, "How was your room? How was the service? How was your stay at the Watergate Hotel?" The groom says, "Why are you asking me all of these questions?" The hotel manager says, "Well, the room under you complained of the chandelier falling on them!"

I just got back from a pleasure trip. I took my mother-in-law to the airport.

A woman is taking a shower. There is a knock on the door. "Who is it?" "Blind man!" The woman is naked but figures, "What the hell, he can't see me anyway." So she opens the door, and the man says, "Lady, where do you want these blinds?"

My son complains about headaches.
I tell him all the time, "Get out of bed feet first!"

My wife is on a new diet—
coconuts and bananas.
She hasn't lost weight,
but she can sure climb a tree!

I've been married 49 years.
Where have I failed?

I've been in love with the same woman for 49 years. If my wife every finds out, she'll kill me!

A guy complains of a headache. Another guy says, "Do what I do. I put my head on my wife's bosom, and the headache goes away." The next day, the man says, "Did you do what I told you?" "Yes, I sure did. By the way, you have a nice house!"

95

I take my wife everywhere, but she keeps finding her way back.

My wife told me the car wasn't running well, there was water in the carburetor. I asked where the car was, and she told me it was in the lake.

I asked my wife, "Where do you want to go for our anniversary?" She said, "Somewhere I have never been!" I told her, "How about the kitchen?"

Another drunk goes up to a parking meter, puts in a quarter, and the dial goes to 60. The drunk says, "Huh. I lost a hundred pounds!"

I'm now making a Jewish porno film. 10 percent sex, 90 percent guilt.

A man goes to a psychiatrist. The doctor says, "You're crazy." The man says, "I want a second opinion!" "OK, you're ugly too!"

A drunk was in front of a judge. The judge says, "You've been brought here for drinking." The drunk says, "OK, let's get started."

Was that suit made to order? Where were you at the time?

My wife will buy anything marked down. Last year she bought an escalator.

She got a mudpack and looked great for two days. Then the mud fell off.

Two guys in a health club, one is putting on pantyhose. "Since when do you wear pantyhose?" "Since my wife found them in the glove compartment!"

I was just in London. There is a six-hour time difference. I'm still confused. When I go to dinner, I feel sexy. When I go to bed, I feel hungry.

A person asked me, "How do you prepare for the stage?" I told her, "Well, it's like this. You go to diction school. They teach you to fill your mouth with marbles and talk right through the marbles. Each day you take one marble out. When you've lost all your marbles..."

She ran after the garbage truck, yelling, "Am I too late for the garbage?" "No, jump in!"

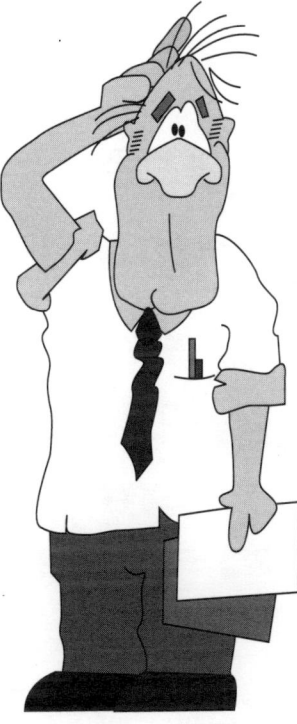

I just finished my income tax forms. Who says you can't get wounded by a blank?

The patient says, "Doctor, it hurts when I do this." "Then don't do that!"

My wife and I have the secret to making a marriage last. Two times a week, we go to a nice restaurant, a little wine, good food..... She goes Tuesdays, I go Fridays.

I know a man who doesn't pay to have his trash collected. How does he get rid of his trash? He gift wraps it and puts in into an unlocked car.

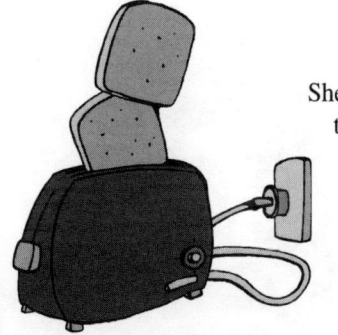

She got an electric blender, electric toaster, electric bread maker. Then she said, "There are too many gadgets and no place to sit down!" So what did I do? I bought her an electric chair.

Kids, do something nice for Mom on Mother's Day... like, move out!

Kids' Jokes

The Trainmaster...

A few days after Christmas a mother was working in the kitchen, listening to her son playing with his new electric train in the living room. She heard the train stop and her son say, "All you sons of bitches who want off, get the hell off now, cause this is the last stop! And all you sons of bitches who are getting on, get your asses into the train, cause we're going down the tracks."

The mother went in to tell her son, "We don't use that kind of language in this house. Now go to your room and stay there for TWO HOURS. When you come out, you may play with your train, but only by using nice language."

Two hours later the son came out of the bedroom and resumed playing with his train. Soon the train stopped and the mother heard her son say, "All passengers who are disembarking the train, please remember to take all of your belongings with you. We thank you for riding with us today and hope your trip was a pleasant one."

She heard the little boy continue, "For those of you just boarding, we ask you to stow all of your hand luggage under your seat. Remember, there is no smoking on the train. We hope you will have a pleasant and relaxing journey with us today."

As the mother began to smile, the child added, "For those of you who are pissed off about the TWO HOUR delay, please see the bitch in the kitchen."

Our parents were never our age.

I was once a millionaire. But my Mom gave away my baseball cards.

Mama, get the hammer! There's a fly on Papa's head.

Deep Young Thoughts...

From a newspaper contest for kids to imitate Saturday Night Live's "Deep Thoughts by Jack Handey."

Give me the strength to change the things I can, the grace to accept the things I cannot, and a great big bag of money.
Age 13

Democracy is a beautiful thing, except for that part about letting any old yokel vote.
Age 10

I bet living in a nudist colony takes all the fun out of Halloween.
Age 13

For centuries people thought the moon was made of green cheese. Then the astronauts found that the moon is really a big hard rock. That's what happens to cheese when you leave it out.
Age 6

As you make your way through this hectic world of ours, set aside a few minutes each day. At the end of the year, you'll have a couple of days saved up.
Age 7

Often, when I am reading a good book, I stop to thank my teacher. That is, I used to, until she got an unlisted number.
Age 15

If we could just get everyone to close his eyes and visualize world peace for an hour, imagine how serene and quiet it would be until the looting started.
Age 15

Kept In The Dark...

Two brothers were riding a train for the first time. They had brought along a bag of bananas for lunch. Just as one bit into his banana, the train entered a tunnel under a mountain. In the darkness was overheard, "Did you take a bite of your banana?"

"No." "Well, don't. I did and I just went blind."

Children's Books You Will NOT See...

You Were an Accident
♥
Strangers Have the Best Candy
♥ ♥
The Little Sissy Who Snitched
♥ ♥ ♥
Some Kittens Can Fly!
♥ ♥ ♥ ♥
Getting More Chocolate on Your Face
♥ ♥ ♥ ♥ ♥
Where Would You Like to Be Buried?
♥ ♥ ♥ ♥ ♥ ♥
Katy Was So Bad Her Mom Stopped Loving Her
♥ ♥ ♥ ♥ ♥ ♥ ♥
The Attention Deficit Disorder Association's Book of Wild Animals of North Amer Hey! Let's Go Ride Our Bikes!
♥ ♥ ♥ ♥ ♥ ♥ ♥ ♥
All Dogs Go to Hell
♥ ♥ ♥ ♥ ♥ ♥ ♥ ♥
The Kids' Guide to Hitchhiking
♥ ♥ ♥ ♥ ♥ ♥ ♥
When Mommy and Daddy Don't Know the Answer, They Say God Did It
♥ ♥ ♥ ♥ ♥ ♥
Garfield Gets Feline Leukemia
♥ ♥ ♥ ♥ ♥
What Is That Dog Doing to That Other Dog?
♥ ♥ ♥ ♥
Why Can't Mr. Fork and Ms. Electrical Outlet Be Friends?
♥ ♥ ♥ ♥
Daddy Drinks Because You Cry
♥ ♥
Mister Policeman Eats His Service Revolver
♥
You Are Different and That's Bad
♥ ♥ ♥ ♥ ♥ ♥ ♥ ♥ ♥ ♥
Why God Burned Down Disneyland

You're Not In College Anymore When...

You're waking up at 6 a.m. instead of going to bed.

College sweatshirts are "casual" instead of dress up.

Your parents charge rent.

Beers at lunch get you reprimanded.

It's "getting late" when it's 9:30 p.m.

You make thousands of dollars a year—and still can't afford that dream Porsche.

You start eyeing the light beer section appreciatively.

Jack and Cokes become Dewers on the rocks.

Pregnancy now brings thoughts of tax deductions instead of coronaries.

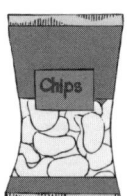

The four food groups are no longer beer, pizza, chips, and cereal.

Pickup football games mean that at least one person will be in the hospital by game's end.

Sneakers are now "weekend shoes."

The only drugs you take are Tums and Tylenol.

Sleeping on the couch is a no-no.

Naps are no longer available between noon and 6 p.m.

Dinner and a movie—the whole date instead of the beginning of one.

The weak single you hit in the intramural softball game is now remembered as a varsity dinger for the league championship.

You get your news from sources other than USA Today, ESPN Sportscenter, and MTV News.

You wear more ties in a week than you even owned in college.

You find yourself reminiscing fondly of two-hour calculus exams.

You empathize with the characters from *Friends*.

You often eat breakfast foods at breakfast time.

Grocery lists actually contain healthy food.

When drinking, you say at least once a night, "I just can't put it down like I used to."

Wine appreciation expands beyond Boone's and Mad Dog.

Over 90 percent of the time you spend in front of a computer is for real work, not video games.

You're willing to pay a bit more to drink in a bar that's not full of 21-year-olds.

Golf is beginning to seem a lot less silly.

We Didn't Do It!

Two brothers in a small town were well known as troublemakers. If there were a problem in town, these boys were guaranteed to be there. Their parents finally decided to do something about it.

They called on the priest. He was known to have success in dealing with problematic behavior. He agreed to see them, but only one brother at a time.

The younger brother went first. He walked in and the priest asked in a mild voice, "Where is God?"

The younger brother just sat there. The priest asked again, "Where's God?" The boy again just sat there, so the priest tried once more, in a very angry voice, "Tell me, son, WHERE IS GOD?"

Terrified, the boy ran out of the church and straight to his room at home, where he hid under the bed. His older brother came in to ask what was wrong.

The younger boy said, "We're in big trouble this time. God is missing, and they think we did it!"

The Quickie...

Bill and Marla decided that the only way to pull off a Sunday afternoon quickie with their 10-year-old son in the apartment was to send him out on the balcony and order him to report on all the neighborhood activities.

The boy began his commentary as his parents put their plan into operation. "There's a car being towed from the parking lot," he said. "An ambulance just drove by." A few moments passed.

"Looks like the Andersons have company," he called out, "Matt's riding a new bike, and the Coopers are having sex."

Mom and Dad shot out of bed. "How do you know that?" the startled father asked.

His son replied, "Their kid is standing on the balcony too."

Little Johnny...

There was a little boy named Johnny who used to hang out at the local corner market. The owner didn't know what Johnny's problem was, but the boys constantly teased him.

They always commented that he was "two bricks shy of a load" or "two pickles short of a barrel." To prove it, sometimes they offered Johnny his choice between a nickel and a dime. He always took the nickel—they said, because it was bigger.

One day after Johnny grabbed the nickel, the store owner took him aside and said "Johnny, those boys are making fun of you. They think you don't know the dime is worth more than the nickel. Are you grabbing the nickel because it's bigger, or what?"

Slowly, Johnny turned toward the store owner. A big grin appeared on his face as Johnny said, "Well, if I took the dime, they'd stop doing it, and so far I've made $20!"

How Old Is She Anyway?

A policeman was patrolling a local parking spot overlooking a golf course. It was almost midnight when he drove by a car and saw a couple inside with the dome light on. There was a young man in the driver's seat reading a computer magazine and a young lady in the back seat knitting. He stopped to investigate.

He walked up to the driver's window and knocked.

The young man looked up, cranked the window down, and said, "Yes, officer?"

"What are you doing?" the policeman asked.

"I'm reading a magazine, Sir." answered the young man.

Pointing toward the young lady in the back seat, the officer asked, "And what's she doing?"

The young man looked over his shoulder and replied, "She's knitting."

"And how old are you?" the officer asked the young man. "I'm 21," he replied.

"And how old is she?" asked the officer.

The young man looked at his watch and said, "Well, in about 12 minutes she'll be 18."

Never Assume Anything With Kids...

A farmer was helping one of his cows give birth when he noticed his four-year-old son standing at the fence, taking in the whole event.

The man thought to himself, "Great... he's four years old, and I'm gonna have to start explaining the birds and bees. No need to jump the gun—I guess I'll wait for him to ask and then I'll answer."

After the calf was born, the man walked over to his son and said, "Well, Son, do you have any questions?"

"Just one," gasped the wide-eyed lad. "How fast was that calf going when it hit that cow?"

What Do The Dogs Do?

A nursery school teacher was delivering a station wagon full of kids home one day when a fire truck zoomed past. Sitting in the front seat of the fire truck was a beautiful spotted Dalmatian.

The children began discussing the dog's duties.

"They use him to keep crowds back," said one youngster.

"No," said another, "he's for good luck."

A third child brought the argument to a close. "They use the dogs," she said firmly, "to find the fire hydrant."

And Now The Priest Streak...

A priest is walking down the street one day when he notices a small boy trying to press a doorbell on a house across the street.

However, the boy is very short and the doorbell is too high for him to reach.

After watching the boy's efforts for some time, the priest moves closer to the boy's position.

He steps smartly across the street, walks up behind the little fellow, and placing his hand kindly on the child's shoulder, leans over, and gives the doorbell a solid ring.

Crouching down to the child's level, the priest smiles benevolently and asks, "And now what, my little man?"

To which the boy replies, "Now we run!"

Afternoon Delight—Beaver Cleaver Days...

It's the spring of 1957 when Bobby goes to pick up his date. He's a pretty hip guy with his own car.

When he rings the front doorbell, the girl's father invites him in. "Carrie's not ready yet, so why don't you have a seat?" he says.

"That's cool," says Bobby. Carrie's father asks Bobby what they're planning to do.

Bobby replies politely that they will probably go to the soda shop or to a movie.

Carrie's father responds, "Why don't you two go out and screw? I hear all the kids are doing it."

Naturally this comes as a quite a surprise to Bobby, so he asks Carrie's dad to repeat.

"Yeah," says Carrie's father, "Carrie really likes to screw; she'll screw all night if we let her!"

Well, this makes Bobby's eyes light up, and his prospects for the evening are looking up.

A few minutes later Carrie bounces downstairs in her little poodle skirt and announces she's ready to go. Almost breathless with anticipation, Bobby eagerly escorts his date to the car.

Twenty minutes later, Carrie rushes back into the house, slams the door behind her, and screams at her father:

"For God's sake, Pops!!! It's called the 'TWIST'!!!"

There is no such thing as justice... In or out of court.

Clarence Darrow

Lawyer Jokes

What Else Is Low-Down, Slippery, and Dangerous?

In Thailand a 27-year-old snake charmer is trying to set a world record by living in a room with a hundred poisonous snakes for a week. The last time this was attempted was at the annual American Bar Association convention.

Criminal Lawyer is a redundancy.

WHY EXPERIMENT ON ANIMALS WITH SO MANY LAWYERS OUT THERE?

99 PERCENT OF LAWYERS GIVE THE REST A BAD NAME.

I Believe You...

There was an attorney who lived in the big city, but he often spent weekends in his cabin in the country. There was a guest room in this cabin, so he frequently asked one of his colleagues or close friends to go up with him each weekend. This particular weekend he had asked his friend, a recent immigrant from the Czech Republic, to go up with him.

When they got there, they basked in the warm spring air, went fishing and berry picking, and relaxed by driving through the quiet countryside. They were picking berries on the second day when they ran into two bears, a male and a female, and obviously the two men had interrupted the bears.

The male bear picked up the lawyer's friend and ate him. Terrified, the lawyer ran the half mile back to his cabin to call the sheriff.

When the sheriff met the lawyer at his cabin, they both went to the site of the tragic attack, and the two bears were still there. "Which one is he in?" asked the sheriff.

"That one," the lawyer said, pointing to the male. So the sheriff shot the female.

"Why did you do that?" cried the lawyer. "I TOLD you, he was in THAT one!"

"Yeah, right," said the sheriff. "Like I'm supposed to believe a lawyer who tells me... the Czech is in the Male."

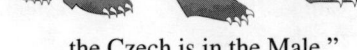

Lawyer, Rabbi, Hindu Joke # 547...

A lawyer and two friends, a Rabbi and a Hindu holy man, had car trouble in the countryside and asked to spend the night with a local farmer.

The farmer said "There may be a problem. I only have room for two in the house, so one of you will have to sleep in the barn." "No problem," said the Rabbi. "My people wandered in the desert for 40 years. I am humble enough to sleep in the barn for a night." With that he left for the barn, and the others bedded down for the night.

Moments later there was a knock at the door. There stood the Rabbi back from the barn. "What's wrong?" asked the farmer. The Rabbi replied, "I am grateful to you, but I cannot sleep in the barn. There is a pig in the barn, and my faith believes that pigs are unclean animals."

The Hindu agreed to swap places with the Rabbi. But a few minutes later the scene recurred. There was a knock on the door. "What's wrong now?" the farmer asked. The Hindu holy man replied, "I too am grateful for your helping us, but there is a cow in the barn, and in my country cows are considered sacred. I cannot sleep where a cow sleeps!"

That left only the lawyer to make the change. He grumbled and complained but headed out to the barn. Moments later there was yet another knock at the farmer's door. Frustrated and tired, the farmer once more got up and opened the door. There stood the pig and the cow!

Language Barrier...

A Mexican bandit made a specialty of crossing the Rio Grande from time to time to rob banks in Texas. Finally, a reward was offered for his capture, and an enterprising Texas ranger decided to track him down. After a lengthy search, he traced the bandit to his favorite cantina, snuck up behind him, put his trusty six-shooter to the bandit's head, and said, "You're under arrest. Tell me where you hid the loot, or I'll blow your brains out."

But the bandit didn't speak English, and the ranger didn't speak Spanish.

Fortunately, a bilingual lawyer was in the saloon and translated the ranger's message. The terrified bandit blurted out—in Spanish—that the loot was buried under the oak tree in back of the cantina.

"What did he say?" asked the ranger.

The lawyer answered, "He said 'Get lost, Gringo. You wouldn't dare shoot me.'"

Be Careful What You Say...

Farmer Joe decided his injuries from the accident were serious enough to take the trucking company (responsible for the accident) to court. In court the trucking company's fancy lawyer was questioning Farmer Joe. "Didn't you say at the scene of the accident, 'I'm fine?'" asked the lawyer. Farmer Joe responded, "Well, I'll tell you what happened. I had just loaded my favorite mule Bessie into the..." "I didn't ask for details," the lawyer interrupted. "Just answer the question. Did you not say at the scene of the accident, 'I'm fine!'"

Farmer Joe said, "Well, I had just got Bessie into the trailer, and I was driving down the road..." The lawyer interrupted again and said, "Judge, I am trying to establish the fact that, at the scene of the accident, this man told the highway patrolman on the scene that he was just fine. Now several weeks after the accident he is suing my client. I believe he's a fraud. Please tell him to answer my question, yes or no."

By this time the judge was getting interested in Farmer Joe's answer, so he said to the lawyer, "I'd like to hear what he has to say about his favorite mule Bessie."

Joe thanked the judge and proceeded, "Well, as I was saying, I had just loaded Bessie, my favorite mule, into the trailer and was driving her down the highway when this huge semitruck and trailer ran the stop sign and smacked my truck right in the side."

"I was thrown into one ditch, and Bessie was thrown into the other. I was hurting real bad and didn't want to move. However, I could hear ole Bessie moaning and groaning. I knew she must be in terrible shape. Shortly after the accident a highway patrolman came on the scene. He could hear Bessie moaning and groaning, so he went over to her. After he looked at her, he took out his gun and shot Bessie between the eyes.

Then the patrolman came across the road with his gun in his hand and looked at me." He said, "Your mule was in such bad shape I had to shoot her. How are you feeling?"

Make It As Tough As Possible, St. Pete...

One day a teacher, a garbage collector, and a lawyer all die and go to Heaven.

St. Peter's having a bad day because Heaven is getting overcrowded. When they get to the gate, St. Peter informs them that there will be an entrance exam. Each will have to answer a single question.

To the teacher he says, "What was the name of the ship that crashed into the iceberg and sank with all its passengers?" The teacher thinks for a second before replying, "That would have been the *Titanic*, right?" St. Peter lets him through the gate.

St. Peter turns to the garbage man, and figuring that Heaven doesn't REALLY need all the stink this guy would bring, decides to make the question a little harder. "How many people on the ship died?" The garbage man guesses, "1228." St. Peter says, "That happens to be right. Come in."

St. Peter then turns to the lawyer and says, "Name them."

Lawyer Joke #269,563...

A lawyer shows up at the Pearly Gates. St. Peter says, "Normally we don't let lawyers in, but you're in luck because this week we're having a special. You go to Hell for the length of time that you were alive, then you get to come back here for eternity."

The lawyer says, "I'll take that deal."

St. Peter says, "Good, I'll put you down for 212 years in Hell..."

The lawyer says, "What are you talking about? I'm only 65 years old!"

St. Peter says, "Up here we go by hours billed."

Body Parts...

A man walking along the beach found a bottle. When he rubbed it, a genie appeared. "I will grant you three wishes," announced the genie. "But there is one condition. I am a lawyer's genie. This means that for every wish you make, every lawyer in the world gets the wish as well—only double." The man thought about this for a while.

"For my first wish, I'd like $10 million," he announced. Instantly the genie gave him a Swiss bank number and assured him that $10 million had been deposited. "But every lawyer in the world has just received $20 million," the genie said.

"I've always wanted a Ferrari," the man said. Instantly a Ferrari appeared. "But every lawyer in the world has just received two Ferraris," the genie said. "What is your last wish?" "Well," said the man, "I've always wanted to donate a kidney for transplant."

If you think talk is cheap, try hiring a lawyer.

What do you have when 100 lawyers are buried up to their necks in sand?
Not enough sand!

In 1381 English peasants revolted. The peasants swore to kill "every lawyer and servant of the king they could find."

So what do you call 10 skydiving lawyers?
Skeet!

Always Planning Ahead...

A young kid walks into a post office one day to see a middle-aged balding man standing at the counter methodically placing "Love" stamps on bright pink envelopes with hearts all over them. He then takes out a perfume bottle and starts spraying scent all over them.

Curiosity gets the better of the kid, so he asks the balding man what he's doing.

The man says, "I'm sending out a thousand Valentines signed, 'Guess who?'"

"But why?" asks the kid, and the man replies, "I'm a divorce lawyer."

The Following Are Actual Statements Made During Court Cases...

The Court: Now, as we begin, I must ask you to banish all present information and prejudice from your minds, if you have any.

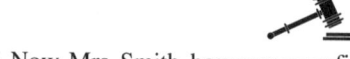

Q. Now, Mrs. Smith, how was your first marriage terminated?
A. By death.
Q. And by whose death was it terminated?

Q. What is your name?
A. Ethel Brown.
Q. And what is your marital status?
A. Fair.

Q. Do you know how far pregnant you are now?
A. I will be three months November 8th.
Q. Let me see. Apparently then, the date of conception was August 8th?
A. Yes.
Q. What were you and your husband doing at that time?

Q. Doctor, how many autopsies have you performed on dead people?
A. All my autopsies have been performed on dead people.

Q. What happened then?
A. He told me, "I have to kill you because you can identify me."
Q. Did he kill you?
A. No.

Q. You say you had three men punching you, kicking you, and raping you, and you didn't scream?
A. No ma'am.
Q. Does that mean you consented?
A. No, ma'am. That means I was unconscious.

Q. When he went, had you gone and had she, if she wanted to and were able, for the time being excluding all the restraints on her not to go, gone also, would he have taken you, meaning you and her, with him to the station?
Mr. Brooks: Objection. That question should be taken out and shot.

Judge: I know you, don't I?
Defendant: Uh, yes.
Judge: All right, tell me, how do I know you?
Defendant: Judge, do I have to tell you?
Judge: Of course. You might be obstructing justice not to tell me.
Defendant: OK, I was your bookie.

Judge: The charge here is theft of frozen chickens. Are you the defendant?
Defendant: No, sir, I'm the guy who stole the chickens.

Lawyer: Tell us about the fight.
Witness: I didn't see no fight.
Lawyer: Well, tell us what you did see.
Witness: I went to a dance at the Turner house, and as the men swung around and changed partners, they slapped each other and one fellow hit harder than the other one liked so the other one hit back and somebody pulled a knife and somebody else drew a six-shooter and another guy came up with a rifle that had been hidden under a bed and the air was filled with yelling and smoke and bullets.
Lawyer: You, too, were shot in the fracas?
Witness: No sir, I was shot midway between the fracas and the navel.

Defendant: Judge, I want you to appoint me another lawyer.
Judge: And why is that?
Defendant: Because the public defender isn't interested in my case.
Judge *(to public defender)*: Do you have any comments on the defendant's motion?
Public Defender: I'm sorry, Your Honor. I wasn't listening.

Defendant *(after being sentenced to 90 days in jail)*: Can I address the court?
Judge: Of course.
Defendant: If I called you a son of a bitch, what would you do?
Judge: I'd hold you in contempt and assess an additional five days in jail.
Defendant: What if I thought you were a son of a bitch?
Judge: I can't do anything about that. There's no law against thinking.
Defendant: In that case, I think you're a son of a bitch.

The patient refused an autopsy.

Medical Jokes

The Top 30 Signs You've Joined A Cheap HMO...

1. Pedal-powered dialysis machines.
2. Use of antibiotics deemed an "unauthorized experimental procedure."
3. Head-wound victim in the waiting room is on the last chapter of *War and Peace*.
4. You ask for Viagra. You get a popsicle stick and duct tape.
5. Your annual breast exam is conducted at Hooters.
6. Exam room has a tip jar.
7. You swear you saw salad tongs and a crab fork on the instrument tray.
8. "Will you be paying in eggs or pelts?"
9. Tight budget prevents acquisition of individual rectal thermometers.
10. "Take two leeches and call me in the morning."
11. The company logo features a hand squeezing a bleeding turnip.
12. Tongue depressors taste faintly like Fudgesicles.
13. Covered postnatal care consists of leaving your baby on Mia Farrow's doorstep.
14. Radiation treatment for cancer patients requires them to walk around with a postcard from Chernobyl.
15. "Prenatal vitamin" prescription is a box of Tic-Tacs.
16. Chief surgeon graduated from University of Benihana.
17. Directions to doctor's office: "Hang a left when you enter trailer park."
18. Doctor listens to your heart through a paper towel tube.
19. Only item listed under Preventive Care Coverage is "An apple a day."
20. Only participating physicians are Dr. Fine, Dr. Howard, Dr. Fine.
21. The only proctologist in the plan is "Gus," from Roto-Rooter.
22. Plan covers only "group" gynecological exams.
23. Preprinted prescription pads say "Walk it off, you sissy."
24. To avoid expensive throat culture, the doctor French kisses you.
25. Recycled bandages.
26. You can get your flu shot as soon as "the" hypodermic needle dries.
27. Your "primary care physician" is wearing pants you donated to Goodwill.
28. Our 24-hour claims line is 1-800-TUF-LUCK.
29. Costly MRI equipment has been replaced by an oversized two-sided copier.
30. Enema? The lavatory faucet swivels to face upward.

Actual Medical Record Quotes As Dictated By Physicians...

The patient reports a burning pain in his penis, which goes to his feet.

By the time he was admitted, his rapid heart had stopped, and he was feeling better.

Patient has chest pain if she lies on her left side for over a year.

On the second day the knee was better and on the third day it had completely disappeared.

She has had no rigors or shaking chills, but her husband states she was very hot in bed last night.

The patient has been depressed ever since she began seeing me in 1983.

I will be happy to go into her GI system. She seems ready and anxious.

The patient is tearful and crying constantly. She also appears to be depressed.

Discharge status: Alive, but without permission. The patient will need disposition, and therefore we will get Dr. Blank to dispose of him.

Healthy-appearing decrepit 69-year-old male, mentally alert but forgetful.

The patient has no past history of suicides.

The patient expired on the floor uneventfully.

The skin was moist and dry.

Occasional, constant, infrequent headaches.

Coming from Detroit, this man has no children.

Patient was released to outpatient department without dressing. I have suggested that he loosen his pants before standing, and then, when he stands with the help of his wife, they should fall to the floor.

Patient was alert and unresponsive.

When she fainted, her eyes rolled around the room.

Patient has left his white blood cells at another hospital.

Patient was becoming more demented with urinary frequency.

She slipped on the ice, and apparently her legs went in separate directions in early December.

The patient experienced sudden onset of severe shortness of breath with a picture of acute pulmonary edema at home while having sex which gradually deteriorated in the emergency room.

The patient left the hospital feeling much better, except for her original complaints.

Between you and me, we ought to be able to get this lady pregnant.

The patient was in his usual state of good health until his airplane ran out of gas and crashed.

Since she can't get pregnant with her husband, I thought you would like to work her up.

She is numb from her toes down.

The patient had waffles for breakfast and anorexia for lunch.

While in the ER, she was examined, X-rated, and sent home.

The patient's past medical history has been remarkably insignificant with only a 40-++pound weight gain in the past three days.

I don't suffer from insanity...
I'm a carrier!

Depression is merely anger without enthusiasm.

Say It Again, Sam...

A stuttering man finally decides to go to the doctor to see if his speech impediment can be cured. The doctor thoroughly examines the man and finally asks him to drop his pants. Out comes this gigantic penis, and the doctor pronounces the root of the problem to be strain on the vocal chords from the effects of gravity being transmitted up to the neck area.

The patient then asks, "Wh-wh-at c-c-ca-an b-b-e d-d-done ab-b-bout-t-t-i-i-t?" to which the doctor replies, "Modern surgery can work miracles. We can replace your penis with one of normal size, and your stuttering will disappear right after the operation."

The patient eagerly agrees to the surgery, and as promised, his stuttering disappears. About three months later the man returns to the doctor to complain, "Doctor, I am grateful to you for having cured me, but my wife really misses a big penis, and rather than lose her, I've decided to get my old penis back. I realize I'll have to live with stuttering for the rest of my life." The doctor then looks straight at the man and replies, "A d-d-de-deal's a d-de-deal."

Never agree to plastic surgery if the doctor's office is full of portraits by Picasso.

Let Me See Your Fingers Too...

A man with a bad stomach goes to his doctor to ask him what he can do. The doctor replies that the illness is serious but can be cured by inserting a suppository up his anus. The man agrees, so the doctor warns him of the pain, tells him to bend over, shoves the thing way up his behind, and works in it thoroughly. The doctor then hands him a second dose and tells him to do the same in six hours.

The man goes home. Later that evening he tries to get the second suppository inserted, but he finds that he cannot reach himself properly to obtain the required depth. He calls his wife over and tells her what to do. The wife nods, puts her hand on his shoulder to steady him, and with the other shoves the medicine home. Suddenly the man screams, "DAMN!" "What's the matter?" asked the wife, "Did I hurt you?"

"No," replies the man, "I just realized that when the doctor did that, he had BOTH hands on my shoulders."

A Trip To The Doctor...

A young mother and her daughter took grandmother to her gynecologist. While she had her feet in the stirrups and the doctor was performing his exam, he remarked, "My, don't we look pretty today."

The lady was quite shocked, but said nothing at the time.

When her daughter picked her up, she was quite upset. This conversation ensued:

Mother: Do you know what that doctor said to me? He said, "Don't we look pretty today," while he was looking between my legs! Do you think that was appropriate?

Daughter: No! Are you sure he wasn't referring to your hairstyle or something?

Mother: Well, it still wasn't appropriate or professional. I wonder if it could be considered sexual harassment. What do you think?

Daughter: I don't know. Were you embarrassed?

Mother: I was very embarrassed. I used some of your FDS this morning, and he may have smelled that, but I still don't think he should have commented!

Daughter: I don't have any FDS.

Mother: Why, certainly you do! In the blue can that was on back of the toilet. I used some before the appointment...

Granddaughter: Oh, Grandmother, that's my *Barbie Golden Glitter Hairspray*.

Doctors, Doctors...

One night as a couple settled into bed, the husband gently tapped his wife on the shoulder and started rubbing her arm. The wife turned over and said, "I'm sorry, honey, I have a gynecologist appointment tomorrow and I want to stay fresh."

Rejected, the husband turned over and tried to sleep. A few minutes later, he rolled back over and tapped his wife again. This time he whispered into her ear, "Do you have a dentist appointment tomorrow too?"

With Viagra such a hit, Pfizer is bringing out a whole line of drugs oriented toward improving men's performance in today's society...

DIRECTRA - A dose of this drug given to men before leaving on car trips caused 72% of them to stop to ask directions when they got lost, compared to a control group of 0.2%.

PROJECTRA - Men given this experimental new drug were far more likely to actually finish a household repair project before starting a new one.

CHILDAGRA - Men taking this drug reported a sudden, overwhelming urge to perform more childcare tasks—especially cleaning up spills and "little accidents."

COMPLIMENTRA - In clinical trials 82% of middle-aged men administered this drug noticed that their wives had a new hairstyle. Currently being tested to see if its effects extend to noticing new clothing.

BUYAGRA - Married and otherwise attached men reported a sudden urge to buy their sweeties expensive jewelry and gifts after talking this drug for only two days. Still to be seen—whether the drug can be continued for a period longer than your favorite store's return policy.

NEGA-VIAGRA - Had the exact opposite effect of Viagra. Undergoing continuing clinical trials on sitting U.S. presidents.

NEGA-SPORTAGRA - This drug had the strange effect of making men want to turn off televised sports and actually converse with other family members.

FLATULAGRA - This complex drug converts men's noxious intestinal gases back into food solids. Special bonus: Dosage can be doubled for long car rides.

FLYAGRA - This drug has been showing great promise in treating men with O.F.D. (Open Fly Disorder). Especially useful for men on Viagra.

PRYAGRA - About to fail its clinical trial, this drug gave men in the test group an irresistible urge to dig into the personal affairs of other people. Note: Apparent overdose turned three test subjects into "Special Prosecutors."

LIAGRA - This drug causes men to be less than truthful when being asked about their sexual affairs. Will be available in ***Regular, Grand Jury,*** and ***Presidential Strength*** versions.

The First Coming...

This man got his first prescription for Viagra and went home to get ready for his wife. His doctor had told him to take it an hour before sex, so he phoned his wife to find out when she would be leaving work. She said, "I'll be home in an hour. He swallowed the pill and waited. An hour passed, the man was ready to go, but his wife did not come.

Then she called him back to say, "Traffic is terrible. I won't be there for another hour."

Frustrated, the man called his doctor, "What should I do?"

"It'd be a shame to waste it," the doctor advised. " Can you can occupy yourself with your housekeeper instead?"

Dismayed the man replied, "Yes, but I don't need Viagra with the housekeeper."

Do you know the difference between Christian women and Jewish women?
Christian women tell their husbands to buy Viagra...
Jewish women tell their husbands to buy Pfizer...

What do you get when you cross Viagra with Rogaine?
Don King!

Following the approval of Viagra by the UK's health authorities, the first shipment arrived yesterday at Heathrow Airport but was hijacked on the way to the pharmacy distribution warehouse. Scotland Yard has warned the public to be on the lookout for a gang of hardened criminals.

If a man overdoses on Viagra, how do they get the casket lid shut?

OF COURSE YOU'VE HEARD ABOUT THE VIAGRA COMPUTER VIRUS.
IT TURNS YOUR 3½-INCH FLOPPY INTO A HARD DISK.

Viagra, medicine's version of MIRACLE-GRO.

Human conception typically involves a chaotic dash by tens of millions of sperm seeking a path to a single egg. Some researchers believe that so many sperm are required because not one of them will stop to ask directions.

Men

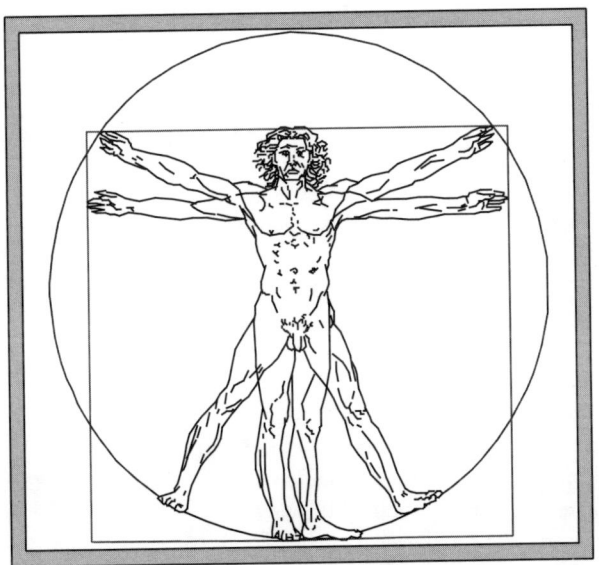

Clothes make the man.
Naked people have little or
no influence on society.

♂♂♂♂♂♂♂

What Are Cats?

FACTS:

They do what they want.
They rarely listen.
They're totally unpredictable.
They whine when they're unhappy.
When you want to play, they want to be left alone.
When you want to be left alone, they want to play.
They expect you to cater to their every whim.
They're moody.
They leave hair everywhere.
They drive you crazy. They cost an arm and a leg.

Conclusion - Cats are tiny little women in cheap fur coats.

WHY IT'S GREAT TO BE A GUY...

1. Phone conversations are over in 30 seconds flat.
2. Movie nudity is virtually always female.
3. A five-day vacation requires only one suitcase.
4. You don't have to monitor your friends' sex lives.
5. Your bathroom lines are 80 percent shorter.
6. You can open all your own jars.
7. Old friends don't give you crap if you've lost or gained weight.
8. Dry cleaners and haircutter's don't rob you blind.
9. When clicking through channels, you don't have to stop on everyone crying.
10. Your ass is never a factor in a job interview.
11. All your orgasms are real.
12. A beer gut does not make you invisible to the opposite sex.
13. You don't have to lug a bag of useless stuff around everywhere you go.
14. You can go to the bathroom without a support group.
15. Your last name stays put.
16. You can leave a hotel bed unmade.
17. When your work is criticized, you don't panic that everyone secretly hates you.
18. You can kill your own food.
19. The garage is all yours.
20. You get extra credit for the slightest act of thoughtfulness.
21. Nobody secretly wonders if you swallow.
22. You never have to clean the toilet.
23. You can be showered and ready in 10 minutes.
24. Having sex doesn't mean worrying about your reputation.
25. Wedding plans take care of themselves.
26. If someone forgets to invite you to something, he or she can still be your friend.
27. Your underwear is $10 for a three-pack.
28. None of your coworkers has the power to make you cry.
29. You don't have to shave below your neck.
30. You don't have to curl up next to a hairy ass every night.
31. If you're 34 and single, nobody notices.
32. You can write your name in the snow.
33. You can get into a nontrivial pissing contest.
34. Everything on your face stays its original color.
35. Chocolate is just another snack.
36. You can quietly enjoy a car ride from the passenger seat.
37. Flowers fix everything.

38. You never have to worry about other people's feelings.
39. You get to think about sex 90 percent of your waking hours.
40. You can wear a white shirt to a water park.
41. Three pairs of shoes are more than enough.
42. You can eat a banana in a hardware store.
43. You can say anything without worrying about what people think.
44. Foreplay is optional.
45. Nobody stops telling a good dirty joke when you walk into the room.
46. You can whip your shirt off on a hot day.
47. You don't have to clean your apartment if the meter reader is coming.
48. You never feel compelled to stop a pal from getting laid.
49. Car mechanics tell you the truth.
50. You don't give a rat's ass if someone notices your new haircut.
51. You and a buddy can watch TV in silence without thinking, "He's mad at me."
52. The world is your urinal.
53. You never misconstrue innocuous statements to mean your lover is about to leave.
54. Hot wax never comes near your pubic area.
55. One mood, all the time.
56. You know at least 20 ways to open a beer bottle.
57. You can sit with your knees apart no matter what you're wearing.
58. Same work... more pay.
59. Gray hair and wrinkles add character.
60. You don't have to leave the room to make an emergency crotch adjustment.
61. If you retain water, it's in a canteen.
62. The remote is yours and yours alone.
63. People never glance at your chest when you're talking to them.
64. You don't have to remember everyones' birthdays and anniversaries.
65. You can drop by to see a friend without taking a little gift.
66. Bachelor parties whomp ass over bridal showers.
67. You can buy condoms without the shopkeeper imagining you naked.
68. Someday you'll be a dirty old man.
69. You can rationalize any behavior with the handy phrase, "F*#k it!"
70. If a guy shows up in the same outfit, you might become lifelong buddies.
71. Not liking a person does not preclude having great sex with her.
72. The occasional well-rendered belch is practically expected.
73. You never have to miss a sexual opportunity because you're not in the mood.
74. Your pals can be trusted never to trap you with, "So... notice anything different?"
75. If something mechanical doesn't work, you can bash it and toss it across the room.
76. Porn movies are designed with your mind in mind.
77. You don't mooch off other people's desserts.
78. There is always a game on somewhere.
79. You know stuff about tanks.
80. Monday Night Football.

Life Is A Series Of Cycles...

When I was in junior high, all I wanted was a girl with big tits.

In high school I dated a girl with big tits, but there was no passion. So I decided I needed a girl with passion.

In college I dated a passionate girl, but she was too emotional. Everything was an emergency. She cried all the time. So I decided I needed a girl with stability.

I found a very stable girl, but she was boring. She never got excited about anything. So I decided I needed a girl with excitement.

I found a very exciting girl, but I couldn't keep up with her. She rushed from one thing to another, never settling on anything. She was directionless. So I decided to find a girl with ambition.

After college I found an ambitious girl and married her. She was so ambitious she divorced me and took everything I owned.

Now all I want is a girl with big tits.

A Similar Theme...

There is a man who has three girlfriends, but he does not know which one to marry. So he decides to give each one $5000 to see how she spends it.

The first one gets a total makeover with the money. She gets new clothes, a new hairdo, manicure, pedicure, the works, and tells the man, "I spent the money so I could look pretty for you because I love you so much."

The second one buys new golf clubs, a CD player, a television, and a stereo and gives them to the man. She says, "I bought these gifts for you with the money because I love you so much."

The third one takes the $5000 and invests it in the stock market, doubles her investment, returns the $5000 to the man and reinvests the rest. She says, "I'm investing the rest of the money for our future because I love you so much."

The man thinks long and hard about how each of the women has spent the money. He decides to marry the one with the biggest breasts.

A Tasty Tidbit?

Our story begins at the Olympics. Specifically it begins at the wrestling event, which has narrowed to the Russian or the American for the gold medal.

Before the final match the American wrestler's trainer tells him, "Now don't forget all the research we've done on this Russian. He's never lost a match because of his 'pretzel' hold. Whatever you do, don't let him get you in that hold! If he does, you're finished!"

The wrestler nods in agreement. The match begins. The American and the Russian circle each other several times, looking for an opening. All of a sudden the Russian lunges forward, grabs the American, and wraps him up in the dreaded pretzel hold! A sigh of disappointment goes up from the crowd, and the trainer buries his face in his hands. He can't watch what he believes to be the end.

Suddenly there is a scream and a cheer from the crowd. The trainer raises his eyes just in time to see the Russian flying through the air. The Russian's back hits the mat with a thud, and the American weakly collapses on top of him, getting the pin, and winning the match.

The trainer is astounded! When he finally gets the American wrestler alone, he asks, "How did you get out of that hold? No one has ever done it before!"

The wrestler answers, "I was ready to give up when at the last moment I opened my eyes and saw testicles right in front of my face."

"I thought I had nothing to lose, so with my last ounce of strength I stretched out my neck and bit those babies just as hard as I could. You'd be amazed what you can do when you crunch into your own balls!"

Things NOT To Say To A Policeman, Guys...

Bad Cop! No Donut!

So, uh, you "on the take," or what?

You're NOT gonna check the trunk, are you?

Hey, you must've been doin' about 125 mph to keep up with me! Good job!

Sorry, Officer, I didn't realize my radar detector was unplugged.

I thought you had to be in relatively good physical condition to be a police officer.

Hi, Officer. Do you mind holding my beer while I find my driver's license?

You know, I was going to be cop, but I decided to finish high school instead.

I was trying to keep up with traffic. Yes, I know there's no other car around. That's how far I was behind the other cars.

Let's do it differently this time. I will give YOU the breathalyzer test. Now stick this into your mouth and blow.

Didn't I see you get your butt kicked on *COPS* last week on TV?

Wow, you look just like the guy in the picture next to my girlfriend's bed.

I bet I could grab that gun before you finish writing my ticket.

Gee, officer! That's terrific. The police officer yesterday only gave me a warning too!

Do you know why you pulled me over? Good, at least one of us does.

Hey, is that a 9 mm? That's nothing compared to this .44 magnum.

Excuse me, is "stick-up" hyphenated?

When you smack the crap outta me, make sure you smile pretty for the video camera.

The Captain...

Long ago when sailing ships ruled the waves, a captain and his crew faced being boarded by pirates. As his crew panicked, the captain bellowed, "Bring me my red shirt!" The first mate quickly retrieved the captain's red shirt, which the captain donned to lead the crew into battle. Although some crew casualties did occur, the pirates were repelled.

Later that day the lookout again screamed that there were pirates on the way. The crew cowered in fear, but the captain again bellowed, "Bring me my red shirt!" The battle raged, and once again the captain and his crew repelled the boarding parties, although this time they suffered more casualties.

Weary from battle, the men sat around on deck that night recounting the day's events. An ensign looked to the captain and asked, "Sir, why did you call for your red shirt before the battle?" The captain, giving the ensign a look that only a captain can give, explained, "If I am wounded in battle, the red shirt does not show the wound and thus, you men will continue to fight unafraid." The men sat in silence, marveling at the courage of such a man.

At dawn the next morning the lookout screamed out a warning of more pirate ships, 10 of them, all on their way with boarding parties. The men became silent and looked to their captain for his usual command.

The captain, calmer than before, bellowed, "Bring me my brown pants!"

The Artist...

An old couple on a tour of the city were visiting an art museum. For the most part they enjoyed themselves with most of the art on display. Eventually they came upon a painting of three naked black men sitting on a bench. The liberal old pair were not offended in the least by the nudity. What they did find perplexing was the fact that the guy on the right had a black penis, the guy on the left had a black penis, but the guy in the middle had a pink penis. They could not figure this out.

As luck would have it, the artist happened to be nearby. He had overheard the old couple talking about his painting. It was obvious they were confused, so he asked them if he could help. They told him that they couldn't understand why the one black man had a pink penis.

The artist explained simply, "You misunderstood the painting. These aren't three black men. They're coal miners. The one in the middle went home for lunch."

If Dear Abby Were A Man...

Dear Mr. Abby:
My husband wants to experience three-in-a-bed-sex with me and my sister.

A: Your husband is clearly devoted to you. He cannot get enough of you, so he goes for the next best thing—your sister. Far from being an issue, this will bring the family together. Why not get some cousins involved? If you are still apprehensive, then let him go with your relatives, buy him a nice expensive present, cook him a delicious meal, and don't mention this aspect of his behavior.

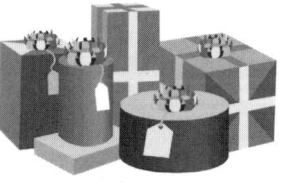

Dear Mr. Abby:
My husband continually asks me to perform oral sex on him.

A: Do it. Sperm is not only great tasting but nutritious. With only 10 calories a spoonful, it helps you keep your figure and gives a great glow to the skin. Interestingly, a man knows this. His offer to you to perform oral sex on him is totally selfless. Oral sex is extremely painful for a man. This shows he loves you. Best thing to do is to thank him, buy him a nice expensive present, and cook him a nice meal.

Dear Mr. Abby:
My husband doesn't know where my clitoris is.

A: Your clitoris is of no concern to your husband. If you must mess with it, do it in your own time. To help with the family budget, you may wish to make a video tape of yourself doing it to sell at flea-markets. To ease your selfish guilt, buy your man a nice expensive present and cook him a delicious meal.

132

Dear Mr. Abby:
My husband is uninterested in foreplay.

A: Foreplay to a man is very hurtful. What it means is that you do not love your man as much as you should—he has to work a lot to get you in the mood. Abandon all wishes in this area, and make it up to him by buying a nice expensive present and cooking a delicious meal.

Dear Mr. Abby:
My husband has too many nights out with the boys.

A: This is perfectly natural behavior—and it should be encouraged. The man is a hunter. He needs to prove his prowess with other men. Far from being pleasurable, a night out with the boys is a stressful affair, and to get back to you is a relief. Just take comfort in how emotional and happy your man is when he returns to his stable home. Best thing to do is to buy him a nice expensive present and cook him a nice meal. Don't mention this aspect of his behavior.

Dear Mr. Abby:
My husband has never given me an orgasm.

A: The female orgasm is a myth. It is a danger to the family unit fostered by militant, man-hating feminists. Don't mention it to him again, and show your love to him by buying a nice expensive present. And don't forget to cook him a delicious meal.

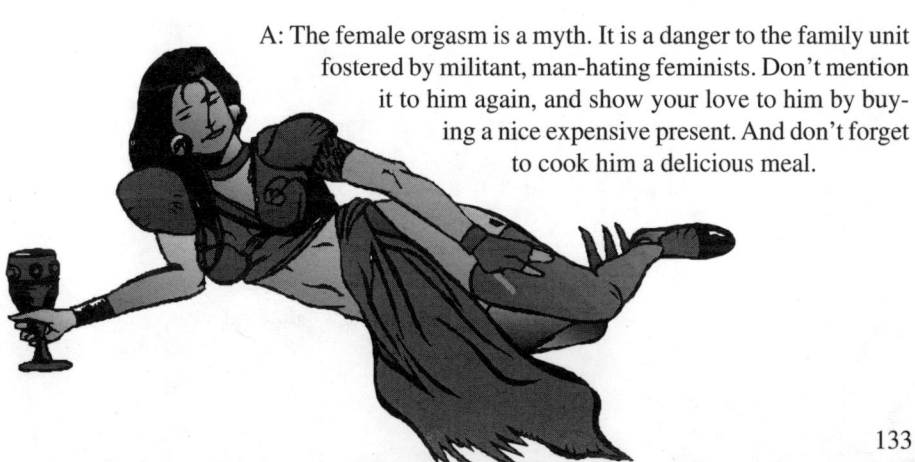

Pass the Main Course...

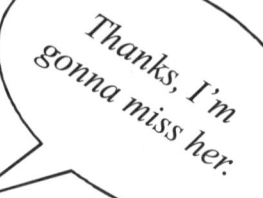

Two cannibal chiefs sat licking their fingers after a large meal. "Your wife makes a delicious roast," one chief said.

Wow, This Might Hurt...

An explorer finds a secluded tribe in the jungle.
He and the chief soon begin comparing cultural differences.

The explorer tells the chief about a peculiar form of bravery called Russian roulette.

The chief says, "We have something similar. Come and see."

The explorer follows the chief to a clearing where a naked man is standing in a circle of six gorgeous naked women.
The chief said, "He has to pick one woman to perform oral sex on him"

The explorer says, "Where's the danger? Where's the bravery?"

The chief says, "One of them is a cannibal!"

Don't be sexist. Broads hate that.

Real men don't waste their hormones growing hair.

HOW DOES AVON FIND SO MANY WOMEN WILLING TO TAKE ORDERS?

THE MORE I LEARN ABOUT WOMEN, THE MORE I LOVE MY CAR.

I GET ENOUGH EXERCISE JUST PUSHING MY LUCK.

Life is sexually transmitted.

WORK IS FOR PEOPLE WHO DON'T KNOW HOW TO FISH.

Hard work has a future payoff. Laziness pays off NOW.

Macho is jogging home after your own vasectomy.

Quick Thinking...

A young hockey player working in a grocery store faces a customer who keeps insisting on buying only half a head of lettuce. Finally, the clerk offers to go to his manager to see what can be done. He begins by explaining, "There's an asshole outside who wants only half a head of lettuce."

Too late he realizes the customer is standing directly behind him and quickly adds, "And this gentleman would like the other half."

After the customer leaves satisfied, the manager congratulates the clerk for his quick thinking and asks, "Where are you from?"

The young man replies, "From Canada, land of two things, hockey players and whores."

Steaming, the manager yells, "My wife's from Canada!"

Instantly the young clerk responds, "Which team?"

The mind is like a parachute. It works best when open.

Miscellaneous

About two decades ago, when Tricky Dick was President, there was a Washington party game to name the thinnest book imaginable, such as Nixon's Morality. Here are some new ones:

Very Thin Books...

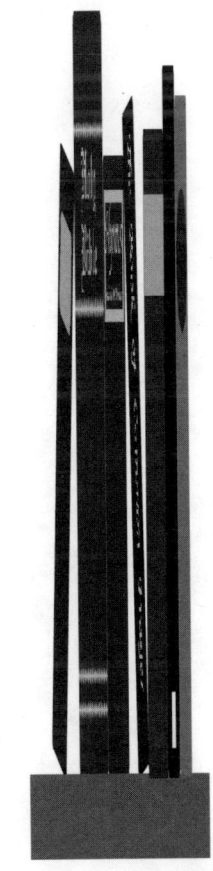

- *Al Gore: The Wild Years*
- *Amelia Earhart's Guide to the Pacific Ocean*
- *America's Most Popular Lawyers*
- *Career Opportunities for History Majors*
- *Detroit: A Travel Guide*
- *Different Ways to Spell "Bob"*
- *Dr. Kevorkian's Collection of Motivational Speeches*
- *Easy UNIX*
- *Ethiopian Tips on World Dominance*
- *Everything Men Know About Women*
- *Everything Women Know About Men*
- *French Hospitality*
- *George Forman's Big Book of Baby Names*
- *How to Sustain a Musical Career,* by Art Garfunkel
- *Mike Tyson's Guide to Dating Etiquette*
- *101 Spotted Owl Recipes,* by the EPA
- *Staple Your Way to Success*
- *The Amish Phone Book*
- *The Engineer's Guide to Fashion*
- *Beating the Legal System*
- *101 Ways to Win with the IRS*
- *You Too Can Beat the Odds at Las Vegas*
- *I Found the Real Killers,* by O.J. Simpson
- *Anyone Can Pick Up Chicks*

Fishing Story...

A keen young lad applied for a sales job in the world's largest department store, which sold almost everything. The boss liked the cut of him and said, "You may start tomorrow. I'll see you at closing time."

It had been a long day. At 5 p.m. the boss stopped by to ask, "How many sales did you make today?" "One," said the new salesman. "Only one," blurted the boss, "Most of my staff make 20 to 30 sales a day. How much was the sale worth?" "It was for $300,000," said the young man.

"How did you manage that?" asked the flabbergasted boss. "Well," said the salesman, "a man came in, and I first sold him a small fish hook. Then I sold him more hooks and some line. When I asked where he was going fishing, he said down the coast. I said he would probably need a boat, so I took him down to the boat department and sold him that 28-foot cabin cruiser with the twin engines. Then he said his present car probably wouldn't be able to pull it, so I took him to the automotive department and sold him a new 4X4 van."

The boss took two steps back and asked in astonishment, "You sold all that to a guy who came in for a fish hook?"

"No," answered the salesman "He came in to buy a box of Tampons for his wife, and I said to him, 'Since your weekend's ruined anyway, you may as well go fishing.'"

Forest Service Comments...

Actual comments left by backpackers completing wilderness camping trips.

"A small deer came into my camp and stole my bag of pickles. Is there a way I can get reimbursed? Please call."

"Escalators would help on steep uphill sections."

"The coyotes made too much noise last night and kept me awake. Please eradicate these annoying animals."

"Trails need to be wider so people can walk while holding hands."

"Trails need to be reconstructed. Please avoid building trails that go uphill."

"Too many rocks in the mountains."

Bagpipe Gags...

Q. How do you make a chain saw sound like a bagpipe?
A. Add vibrato.

Q. What's the difference between a dead snake in the road and a dead bagpiper in the road?
A. Skid marks in front of the snake.

Q. What's the range of a bagpipe?
A. Twenty yards if you have a good arm.

Q. Why are bagpipers fingers like lightning?
A. They rarely strike the same spot twice.

Q. What's the difference between a bagpipe and an onion?
A. No one cries when you chop up a bagpipe.

Q. What's the difference between a lawn mower and a bagpipe?
A. You can tune the lawn mower.

Q. What's the definition of a gentleman?
A. Someone who knows how to play the bagpipe—and doesn't.

Q. What's the difference between a dead bagpiper in the road and a dead country singer in the road?
A. The country singer may have been on the way to a recording session.

Q. How can you tell if a bagpipe is out of tune?
A. Someone is blowing into it.

If you took all the bagpipers in the world and laid them end to end—it would be a good idea.

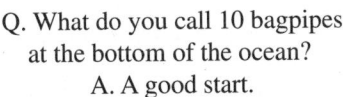

Q. What do you call 10 bagpipes at the bottom of the ocean?
A. A good start.

Q. Why do bagpipers walk when they play?
A. To get away from the sound.

Q. What's the definition of "optimism"
A. A bagpiper with a beeper.

Be Careful How You Say It...

A man goes into a restaurant and sits down at a table. When the homely waitress asks for his order, he replies, "I want a quickie."

She slaps his face and barks, "Now would you please give me your order." Again, he says, "I want a quickie." She slaps him again and yells, "I'll give you one last chance! What do you want?"

Someone from the next table leans over and whispers, "I think it's pronounced *quiche*."

Memory...

An elephant is drinking at a river when he spots a turtle asleep on a log. The elephant ambles over and kicks the unsuspecting turtle clear across the river.

"Why did you do that?" asks a giraffe.

"Because I recognized it as the same turtle that took a nip out of my trunk 47 years ago."

"Wow, what a memory!" says the giraffe.

"Yes," says the elephant, "turtle recall."

Gotcha!

A mother with her small child was trying to hail a cab in New York City. Her daughter noticed several wildly-dressed women loitering on a nearby street corner. The mother got a cab and they both climbed in, at which point the daughter asked, "Mummy, what are all those ladies waiting for by that corner?" The mother replied, "Those ladies are waiting for their husbands to come home from work, dear."

The cabbie, on hearing this exchange, turned to the mother and said, "Ahhhhhhh, C'mon lady! Tell your daughter the truth, fer crying out loud! They're hookers!"

An angry silence settled on the speeding cab, broken by the daughter asking, "Mummy, do the, er, hookers have any children?" The mother calmly replied, "Of course, dear. Where do you think cabbies come from?"

Puns...

As the shopper placed her groceries on the checkout stand, the bagger asked, "Paper or plastic?" "Doesn't matter" she replied, "I'm bisackual."

I took my four-year-old son to see the latest Disney movie. Before the feature there was a Donald Duck cartoon. When my son got up and asked to be excused, I asked him why. He told me Donald Duck always gives him Disneyspells.

An ace British aviator was knighted by Queen Elizabeth. Whenever he flew over Buckingham Palace, he dipped his wings in salute. The Queen was asked, "Who's that pilot?" She replied, "That's the fly-by knight!"

Show me a blacksmith who is making hardware for a bathroom, and I'll how you a man who is forging a head.

A one-L lama is a Tibetan priest.
A two-L llama is a South American beast of burden.
A three-L lllama is a helluva fire.

The wife of a Las Vegas doctor telephoned a local casino and asked to have her husband paged. "Sorry, Madam," came the reply. "The house does not make doctor calls"

Betsy Ross asked a group of colonists for their opinions of the flag that she had made. It was the first flag poll.

When the first marble building was constructed, everyone took it for granite.

William Canby is credited with having invented the first computing scales, which proves that where there's a Will, there's a weigh.

Every successful department store knows that elevators have their ups and downs, but escalators are a step in the right direction.

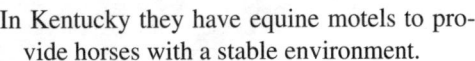

In Kentucky they have equine motels to provide horses with a stable environment.

The inventor of artificial snow originally called his product Snow Fakes.

The Janitors Union went on strike demanding sweeping reforms. The Baker's Union, however, wanted more dough.

When the first calendar was produced in 1640, everyone realized his days were numbered.

> I've sometimes thought of marrying, and then I've thought again.
> — Noel Coward

Movies

30 Things You'd Never Know Without The Movies...

1. The ventilation system of any building is the perfect hiding place. No one will ever think of looking for you there, and you can travel to any other part of the building without difficulty.

2. It's not necessary to speak German in order to pass yourself off as a German officer. Something approximating a German accent will do.

3. A man will show no pain while taking the most ferocious beating, but he will wince when a woman tries to clean his wounds.

4. Kitchens don't have light switches. When entering a kitchen at night, open the refrigerator door and use that light instead.

5. All telephone numbers in America begin with the digits 555.

6. All beds have special L-shaped cover sheets that reach up to the armpits of a woman but only to the waist of the man lying beside her.

7. If staying in a haunted house, women should investigate all strange noises in their most revealing underwear.

8. Cars that crash will almost always burst into flames.

9. Wearing a tattered T-shirt or stripping to the waist renders a man practically invulnerable to bullets.

10. If you find yourself caught up in a misunderstanding that could be cleared up quickly with a simple explanation, it's more dramatic to keep your mouth shut.

11. A cough is usually the sign of a terminal illness.

12. All bombs are fitted with electronic timing devices with large red readouts so you know exactly when they're ready to go off.

13. When in love, it's customary to burst into song.

14. When confronted by an evil international terrorist, sarcasm and wisecracks are your best weapons.

15. One man shooting at 20 men has a better chance of killing all of them than 20 men have of shooting one man.

16. Creepy music coming from a cemetery should always be investigated closely.

17. Most laptop computers are powerful enough to override the communication systems of any invading alien civilization.

18. Freelance helicopter pilots are always eager to accept bookings from international terrorist organizations, even though the job requires them to shoot total strangers before their own certain death as the helicopter explodes in a ball of flames.

19. Most people keep scrapbooks of newspaper clippings—especially if any of their family or friends has died in a strange boating accident.

20. All computer disks will work in all computers regardless of software.

21. Police departments give their officers personality tests to ensure they assign partners who are total opposites.

22. When they're alone, all foreigners prefer to speak English to each other.

23. Action heroes never face charges for manslaughter or criminal damage, despite laying entire cities to waste by their actions.

24. You can always find a chainsaw when you need one.

25. Any lock can be picked by a credit card or a paper clip in seconds—unless it's the door to a burning building with a child trapped inside.

26. You can tell if a man is British because he'll be wearing a bow tie.

27. Having a job of any kind will make a father forget his son's eighth birthday.

28. Honest hardworking policemen are traditionally gunned down three days before their retirement.

29. If a woman is blonde and pretty, it is possible for her to become a world expert in nuclear fission at age 22.

30. The more a man and woman hate each other, the more likely they are to fall in love.

Quotable Quotes...

Smoking kills. If you're killed,
you've lost a very
important part of your life.
*Brooke Shields, during an interview
to become spokesperson for a
federal antismoking campaign*

Many a man owes
his success to his first wife
and his second wife to his success.
Jim Backus

She's a lovely person.
She deserves a good husband.
Marry her before she finds one.
*Oscar Levant to Harpo Marx
upon meeting Harpo's fiancée*

A successful man
is one who makes more money
than his wife can spend.
A successful woman is one who can find such a man.
Lana Turner

If it weren't for electricity, we'd all be watching television by candlelight.
George Gobel

Now they show you how detergents take out bloodstains—
a pretty violent image there.
I think if you've got a T-shirt with a bloodstain all over it,
maybe laundry isn't your biggest problem.
Maybe you should get rid of the body before you do the wash.
Jerry Seinfeld

I always wanted to be somebody,
but I should have been more specific.
Lily Tomlin

Possible Hollywood Headlines...

Madonna's Record Threatened - Saxophonist Kenny G will attempt to blow a note for more than 15 minutes, a new Guinness record on December 1st in NYC.

No One Complained About Marilyn Monroe - The Bugs Bunny stamp, the first ever to honor a cartoon character, debuted in a first-day issue at CA's Burbank Post Office. It's being criticized for dumbing-down and commercializing America's stamp heritage.

Whacko Jacko Back In Racko? - British tabloid *The Daily Star* says Michael Jackson's wife Debbie Rowe is pregnant again.

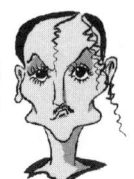

Look At The Pair On Snow White - Disney characters Donald Duck and Joe Carioca led off Rio's first Carnival parade, replacing traditional barebreasted G-stringed girls. Disney had agreed to funding only if the nudity were eliminated.

Called *On Our Backs* - Christie Brinkley, four-times-married, will host a cable show on *Lifetime* about celebrity weddings.

The Nutty Cross-Dresser - Eddie Murphy spent the weekend on TV insisting he was only "offering a friendly ride" to a transvestite prostitute he picked up after midnight Thursday. An antiprostitution patrol car saw them, stopped him, and booked the rider on outstanding warrants. No charges on Murphy.

Like *CATS*, Except Good Songs - Disney Pictures announced it'll produce *The Lion King* as a live musical at its new Times Square theater.

Only On Dress-Down Fridays - Emmy-winning talk show host Montel Williams is being sued for sexual harassment by two former female employees who claim that, among other gross acts, he also conducted meetings in his underwear.

Plus Free Home Bleaching - Michael Jackson married Debbie Rowe, his plastic surgeon's nurse, who is carrying his baby.

His Copies Of *Boy's Life* - Following Michael Jackson's departure, a New Zealand hotel auctioned off his room's blankets, pillowcases, bathrobe, and leftover M&Ms. Proceeds to charity.

Don't Touch Me There - Fitness personality Richard Simmons announced he'll go to medical school to become a doctor.

I base most of my fashion taste on what doesn't itch.
Gilda Radner

Wow, $6.25 Million Each:

Demi Moore's movie *Striptease* opened to terrible reviews but considerable male glandular excitement. Her $12.5 million is the biggest movie payday ever for an actress.

**Between two evils,
I always pick the one I've never tried before.**
Mae West

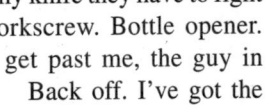

The Swiss have an interesting army. Five hundred years without a war. Pretty impressive. Also pretty lucky for them. Ever see that little Swiss Army knife they have to fight with? Not much of a weapon there. "Come on, buddy, let's go. You back of me, he's got a spoon. toe clippers right here."
Jerry Seinfeld

Corkscrew. Bottle opener. get past me, the guy in Back off. I've got the

Some Priceless Gems By Rodney Dangerfield...

If it weren't for pickpockets, I'd have no sex life at all.

One day as I came home early from work, I saw a guy jogging naked. I said to the guy, "Hey buddy, why are you doing that?" "He said, Because you came home early."

Its been a rough day. I got up this morning, put on a shirt, and a button fell off. I picked up my briefcase, and the handle came off. I'm afraid to go to the bathroom.

When I played in the sandbox, the cat kept covering me up.

I could tell that my parents hated me. My bath toys were a toaster and a radio.

My mother never breastfed me. She told me that she only liked me as a friend.

My father carries around the picture of the kid that came with his wallet.

When I was born, the doctor came out to the waiting room and said to my father, "I'm very sorry. We did everything we could. But he pulled through."

My mother had morning sickness—after I was born.

I remember the time I was kidnapped, and they sent a piece of my finger to my father. He said he wanted a lot more proof.

Once when I was lost, I saw a policeman and asked him to help me find my parents. I said to him, "Do you think we'll ever find them?" He said, "I don't know, kid. There are so many places they can hide."

I went to the doctor because I'd swallowed a bottle of sleeping pills. My doctor told me to have a few drinks and get some rest.

I'm an excellent housekeeper.
Every time I get divorced I keep the house.
Zsa Zsa Gabor

I'm not offended by all the dumb blonde jokes because
I know I'm not dumb—
and I also know that I'm not blonde.
Dolly Parton

Sometimes I wonder if men and women really suit each other.
Perhaps they should live next door and just visit now and then.
Katherine Hepburn

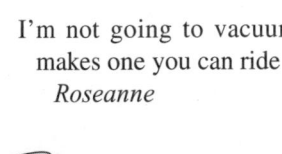

I'm not going to vacuum 'til Sears
makes one you can ride on.
Roseanne

A man is incomplete until he is married.
After that, he's finished.
Zsa Zsa Gabor

I don't date women my age. There aren't any.
Milton Berle

The trouble with life is—
by the time you can read a
girl like a book,
your library card
has expired.
Milton Berle

I have everything
I had 20 years ago.
Only it's a little
bit lower.
Gypsy Rose Lee

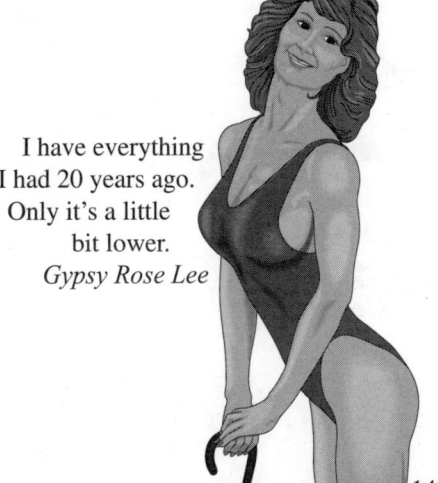

You have the right to remain silent. Anything you say will be misquoted, then held against you.

News

Good Humor—Bad Ads...
Actual classified ads from actual classified sections of actual newspapers:

Two female Boston Terrier puppies, seven wks old, 555-1234. Leave mess.

Lost: Small apricot poodle. Reward. Neutered. Like one of the family.

A superb and inexpensive restaurant. Fine food expertly served by waitresses in appetizing forms.

Dinner Special: Turkey $2.35; Chicken or Beef $2.25; Children $2.00.

For Sale: Antique desk suitable for lady with thick legs and large drawers.

Four-Poster Bed, 101 years old. Perfect for antique lover.

Now is your chance to have your ears pierced and get an extra pair to take home too.

Wanted: 50 girls for stripping machine operators in factory.

Wanted: Unmarried girls to pick fresh fruit and produce at night.

We do not tear your clothing with machinery. We do it carefully by hand.

For Sale: Three canaries of undermined sex.

For Sale: Eight puppies from a German Shepherd and an Alaskan Hussy.

Great Dames for sale.

Have several very old dresses from grandmother in beautiful condition.

Tired of cleaning yourself? Let me do it.

Dog for Sale: Eats anything and is fond of children.

Vacation Special: Have your home exterminated.

Mt. Kilimanjaro, the breathtaking backdrop for the Serena Lodge. Swim in the lovely pool while you drink it all in.

Get rid of aunts: Zap does the job in 24 hours.

Toaster: A gift that every member of the family appreciates. Automatically burns toast.

Sheer Stockings: Designed for fancy dress, but so serviceable that lots of women wear nothing else.

For Rent: 6-room hated apartment. Man, honest. Will take anything.

Wanted: Chambermaid in rectory. Love in, $200 a month. References required.

Man wanted to work in dynamite factory. Must be willing to travel.

Used Cars: Why go elsewhere to be cheated? Come here first!

Christmas Tag-Sale: Handmade gifts for the hard-to-find person.

Wanted: Haircutter. Excellent growth potential.

Wanted: Man to take care of cow that does not smoke or drink.

3-year-old teacher for preschool. Experience preferred.

Our experienced Mom will care for your child. Fenced yard, meals, and smacks included.

Our bikinis are exciting. They are simply the tops.

Auto Repair Service: Free pickup and delivery. Try us once, you'll never go anywhere again.

Illiterate? Write today for free help.

Girl Wanted to assist magician in cutting-off-head illusion. Blue Cross and salary.

Wanted: Widower with school-age children requires person to assume general housekeeping duties. Must be capable of contributing to growth of family.

And Now, the Superstore—unequaled in size, unmatched in variety, unrivaled inconvenience.

We Will Oil your sewing machine and adjust tension in your home for $1.00.

All The News That Fits...

*The Graduate School of Journalism at Columbia University
annually lists the most arresting headlines of the year.
These are real, gleaned from newspapers around the country:*

Include Your Children When Baking Cookies
Something Went Wrong In Jet Crash, Experts Say
Police Begin Campaign To Run Down Jaywalkers
Safety Experts Say School Bus Passengers Should Be Belted
Drunk Gets Nine Months In Violin Case
Survivor of Siamese Twins Joins Parents
Iraqi Head Seeks Arms
Prostitutes Appeal to Pope
Panda Mating Fails; Veterinarian Takes Over
British Left Waffles On Falkland Islands
Lung Cancer In Women Mushrooms
Eye Drops Off Shelf
Teachers Strike Idle Kids
Clinton Wins On Budget, But More Lies Ahead
Enraged Cow Injures Farmer With Axe
Plane Too Close To Ground, Crash Probe Told
Miners Refuse To Work After Death
Juvenile Court To Try Shooting Defendant
Stolen Painting Found By Tree
Two Sisters Reunited After 18 Years In Checkout Counter
Killer Sentenced To Die For Second Time In 10 Years
Never Withhold Herpes Infection From Loved One
War Dims Hope For Peace
If Strike Isn't Settled Quickly, It May Last A While
Cold Wave Linked To Temperatures
Deer Kill 17,000
Enfields Couple Slain; Police Suspect Homicide
Red Tape Holds Up New Bridges
Typhoon Rips Through Cemetery; Hundreds Dead
Man Stuck By Lightning Faces Battery Charge
New Study Of Obesity Looks For Larger Test Group
Astronaut Takes Blame For Gas In Spacecraft
Kids Make Nutritious Snacks
Chef Throws His Heart Into Helping Feed Needy
Arson Suspect Held In Massachusetts Fire
Ban On Soliciting Dead In Trotwood
High School Dropouts Cut In Half
New Vaccine May Contain Rabies
Hospitals Are Sued By Seven-Foot Doctors

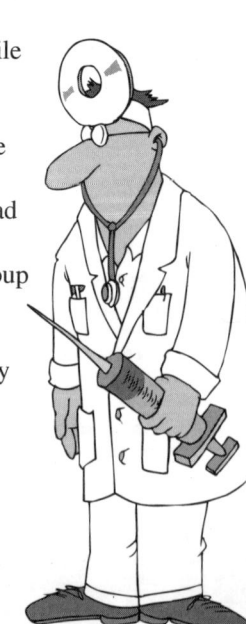

Science Project Fools Sniffing Dog...

BOWLING GREEN, OH—Wolfgang the drug-sniffing dog got tripped up by an "Earth Ball." Wolfgang alerted authorities that there was something suspicious in 13-year-old Dylan Brill's locker during a 1,000-locker drug search at Bowling Green Junior High School. Police found a plastic bag filled with a weird green material. Two weeks later, they finally found out what it was: the boy's four-month-old science project. He had mixed the laundry detergent Borax with white glue, green paint, and water for a "Save The Earth" project. The substance was tested twice for marijuana, barbiturates, cocaine and amphetamines. Both came back inconclusive. "The only thing Dylan is guilty of is having a messy locker," said the boy's mother, Gwen Brill.

Doggone Those Police...

RANTOUL, IL—Intruders had the run of a local pharmacy until the police put an end to their freedom. Police were investigating a possible break-in at a Revco Drug Store after a witness reported movement in the store. It turned out to be a pair of chocolate-colored Labrador retrievers. According to the police report, employees had forgotten to lock the store when they went home. The stray dogs stepped onto the automatic door mats, which opened the doors, and trotted inside. When police tried to chase the dogs, they ran out of the drugstore and into a 24-hour grocery store next door. Police captured the unlucky dogs in the grocery store and took them to the Rantoul Municipal Pound.

Bare Wares...

AMHERST, OH—The naked mannequins in Tom Baker's storefront have raised a few eyebrows. "They're pretty graphic," Amherst Trustee Dan Jackson said. Baker restores and sells used store mannequins. Last fall the town's three trustees told him that at least six people had complained about his unclad mannequins. Baker removed the non-anatomically-correct mannequins at first but recently put them back on display. "One trustee asked me to dress them—but I'm not in the clothing business," Baker said. "If I dressed them, then people would think this is a clothing store and walk by."

Police Chase In Reverse...

SAN JOSE, CA—A motorist who was pulled over for a carpool lane violation tried to back over the trooper who stopped him, then chased the motorcycle officer on a freeway at speeds up to 100 mph. The fleeing California highway patrol trooper was forced to weave in and out of traffic on busy Highway 17 to evade the driver, who eventually crashed into a guard rail and suffered minor injuries. Art Riven was being held on suspicion of attempted murder of a police officer, assault with a deadly weapon—his car—against an officer, and evading arrest. He had no prior driving citations and there was no indication of drugs or alcohol. "We don't know what he was thinking. He won't talk to us," a patrol spokesman said.

Excuse Me, But You're Under Arrest...

GARY, IN—Police say Randy Atkins, 18, had a question: "Can I have all of your money please?" "No, I don't have any money," answered Doug Gibson of Irving, NY. So Atkins got back into a car with three men and left. Gibson saw the license plate on the car and called police, who arrested the men minutes later. Atkins, who was identified as the "polite robber," was charged with carrying a gun without a permit and armed robbery. The other three also were charged with armed robbery.

Real Holes In Robber's Plan...

Tips for robbing the doughnut shop where you once worked:

1. Do disguise your voice.
2. Don't let your accomplice call you by your real name.
3. Don't leave a trail of coins leading to your apartment.

NORTHBRIDGE, MA—Police said a former Dunkin' Donuts employee was arrested and charged with armed robbery and assault. Two masked men brandishing a tire iron and hatchet broke into the shop around 1 a.m., striking an employee. Police said Alonso J. Romano, 18, admitted taking part in the robbery after they followed a trail of coins and footprints to his apartment building, two doors down from the shop. Police said they found more than $1,400 in cash, two ski masks, a tire iron, and a hatchet. The injured employee also told police he recognized Romano's voice, especially after the other man called him "A.J.," his nickname. Police said they expected to arrest the second man.

Nothing Good On Any Of Them...

MONTESANO, WA—Fourteen-year-old Linda West won 100 televisions in ABC's "I Celebrate TV" contest. The family has accepted 70 so far. There was no option of taking cash. Linda entered the contest through the Internet, and the eighth-grader was a little dubious when told she'd won. "I thought it was one of those Publishers Clearing House things—you know, with the 'You may have won letters,'" she said. Any doubts vanished when the sets began arriving. The TVs, by various manufacturers, included two 61-inch sets, several 35-inch sets, and a lot of 20- and 13-inch sets. The retail value is about $31,000. The family hopes to sell most of the sets.

Justice Can Be Smelly...

ALBANY, NY—Police said Nick Charles III parked a pickup truck outside the state's highest court and sprayed the columned building with liquefied chicken manure. Firemen hosed down the building, and the area was sprayed with disinfectant said Paul Downing, a spokesman for the court of appeals. But it was evident more cleanup work was needed. "It smells like a Hong Kong chicken farm in July, not a court in winter," he said. Charles said he wanted to get arrested to publicize what he calls rampant corruption in the courts. He is charged with second-degree criminal mischief, a felony that carries punishment of up to seven years in prison.

Bill And GM...

At a recent COMDEX show Bill Gates reportedly compared the computer industry with the auto industry stating, "If GM had kept up with technology like the computer industry has, we would all be driving $25 cars that get 1,000 miles a gallon."

Recently General Motors addressed this comment by releasing the statement "Yes, but would you want your car to crash twice a day?"

Will The Real Dummy Please Stand Up?

NEW YORK, NY—AT&T fired President John Watkins after nine months, saying he lacked "intellectual leadership." He received a $26 million severance package.

Who lacked intelligence?

With A Little Help From Our Friends!

OAKLAND, CA—Police spent two hours attempting to subdue a gunman who had barricaded himself inside his home. After firing 10 tear gas canisters, officers discovered that the man was standing beside them, shouting pleas to come out and give himself up.

And These Nitwits Are Teaching Our Children?

MANASSAS, VA—A nine-year-old boy received a one-day suspension under his elementary school's drug policy last week—for eating Certs! Joey Hoeffer allegedly told a classmate that the mints would make him "jump higher."

BELLE, WV—A student was suspended for three days for giving a classmate a cough drop. School principal Forest Mann reiterated the school's "zero-tolerance" policy, which should not be confused with the "zero-intelligence" policy.

And What Was Plan B?

CHICAGO, IL—A local man pretending to have a gun kidnapped a motorist and forced him to drive to two different automated teller machines. The kidnapper then proceeded to withdraw money from his own bank accounts.

Some Days, It Just Doesn't Pay To Gnaw Through The Straps...

MAUI, HA—Fire investigators have determined the cause of a blaze that destroyed a $127,000-home last month—a short in the homeowner's newly installed fire prevention alarm system. "This is even worse than last year," said the distraught homeowner, "when someone broke in and stole my new security system."

And For The Main Course...

TAORMINA, ITALY—A local man was hospitalized after swallowing 46 teaspoons, two cigarette lighters, and a pair of salad tongs.

The Getaway...

TOPEKA, KS—A man walked into a Kwik Shop and asked for all the money in the cash drawer. Apparently the take was too small, so he tied up the store clerk and worked the counter himself for three hours until police showed up and grabbed him.

Have I Got a Deal for You!

ROME, ITALY—According to Italian police, more than six hundred people wanted to ride in a spaceship badly enough to pay $10,000 each for the first tourist flight to Mars. The would-be space travelers were told they could, "Spend their next vacation on Mars amid the splendors of ruined temples and painted deserts. Ride a Martian camel from oasis to oasis and enjoy the incredible Martian sunsets. Explore mysterious canals and marvel at the views. Trips to the moon also available." Authorities believe the con men running this scam made off with over $6 million dollars.

Did I Say That?

LOS ANGELES, CA—Police had good luck with a robbery suspect who couldn't control himself during a lineup. When detectives asked each man in the lineup to repeat the words, "Give me all your money or I'll shoot," the man shouted, "That's not what I said!"

Ouch, That Smarts!

VIRGINIA BEACH, VA—A bank robber got a nasty surprise when a dye pack designed to mark stolen money exploded in his Fruit-of-the-Looms underwear. The robber had apparently stuffed the loot down the front of his pants as he was running out of the bank's door. Police spokesman Mike Barry reported, "After the explosion inside his pants, he was observed hopping and jumping around." Police have both the man and his charred trousers in custody.

IF YOU DON'T LIKE THE NEWS, GO OUT AND MAKE SOME.

That Really Sucks...

SEATTLE, WA—When a man attempted to siphon gasoline from a motor home parked on a local street, he got much more than he bargained for. Police arrived at the scene to find the thief curled up sick next to the motor home. A police spokesman said that the thief admitted trying to steal gasoline but plugged his hose into the motor home's sewage tank by mistake. The owner of the vehicle declined to press charges, saying that it was the best laugh he'd ever had.

Cell Phone Come-On...

NEW YORK, NY—When a woman reported her car stolen, she mentioned to police that it had a car phone. The policeman taking her report then called the car phone and told the guy who answered that he had read his ad in the newspaper and wanted to buy the car. He made an appointment to see the car and arrested the thief.

A Penny For Your Thoughts...

PROVIDENCE, RI—A young man from the suburbs knocked out an armored car driver and stole four bags of money. It turned out they contained $800 in PENNIES. Each bag weighed 30 pounds, which slowed him to a stagger during his getaway so that police officers easily jumped him from behind.

Oops!

PONTIAC, MI—A drug-possession defendant on trial in March claimed he had been searched without a warrant. The prosecutor said the officer didn't need a warrant because a bulge in the defendant's jacket might have been a gun. "Nonsense," said the defendant, who happened to be wearing the same jacket that day in court. He handed it over to the judge for examination. The judge discovered a packet of cocaine in the pocket and laughed so hard he needed a five-minute recess to compose himself.

How Do You Spell "Gas" Anyway?

EL PASO, TX—Clever drug traffickers used a propane tanker truck from Mexico that they rigged to release propane gas from all of its valves. In fact, the truck concealed 6,240 pounds of marijuana. The crooks were clever, but not bright. They misspelled the name of the gas company on the side of the truck.

THERE ARE THREE KINDS OF PEOPLE: THOSE WHO CAN COUNT & THOSE WHO CAN'T.

Dumb And Dumber...

OKLAHOMA CITY—A young Oklahoma man fired his lawyer this week during a trial for armed robbery of a convenience store. The assistant district attorney said the amateur attorney was doing a fair job of defending himself until the store manager fingered him as the robber. The defendant jumped up, accused the female manager of lying, and yelled, "I should of blown your [expletive] head off." The defendant paused then quickly added, "If I'd been the one who was there." The jury took 20 minutes to convict the defendant-lawyer and recommend a 30-year sentence.

How Do You Spell "Fugitive?"

DETROIT, MI—An inquisitive pedestrian walked up to two patrol officers who were showing their new squad car computer equipment to children in a downtown neighborhood. When he wanted to see how the system worked, the officers asked him for an ID. Using his driver's license, they entered the number into their computer. Moments later they arrested their visitor when screen information showed he was wanted for a two-year-old armed robbery in St. Louis, MO.

FORGET ABOUT WORLD PEACE... VISUALIZE USING YOUR TURN SIGNAL.

Twist And Shout...

MOMBASSA, KENYA—A local couple required police and medical assistance to get untangled after "becoming stuck" while making love. The Kenya *Times* reported that police had to fire tear gas to disperse a crowd of hundreds of curious onlookers. The lovers were airlifted to Nairobi to be separated. Doctors suggested tension and excitement may have been factors.

MAKE IT IDIOT-PROOF AND SOMEONE WILL MAKE A BETTER IDIOT.

OCALA, FL—A local restaurant was robbed last month by a man wearing only a pair of boxer shorts—on his head.

FORGET THE JONESES, I KEEP UP WITH THE SIMPSONS.

Rhyming Headlines Hall of Fame...

These are from the very funny daily A.M. NEWS ABUSE reports:

French Wench In Trench Stench Monkey Wrench - A Paris court ordered the exhumation of star Yves Montand for DNA tests. It will be used to verify a woman's claim she is his daughter. The actor-singer, who died in 1970, is buried next to his first wife, actress Simone Signoret. While alive he refused all DNA tests.

Cleavage Give Sleevage The Heavage - Beleaguered Guess is dropping its fully-clothed ad motif, which showed actual Guess products, and is returning to the ads that made them a force in the first place—Claudia Schiffer-types in bustiers.

Thousands Fail Low-Crawl Maneuvers - The Pentagon revealed its 1999 Viagra expenses for American troops and retirees will top $50 million. Costs might reach $100 million if they gave it to every serviceman requesting it (which they say they won't).

Corps Pore O'er Poor Whore Spoors - Researchers have discovered a small pocket of about 60 indigent prostitutes in Kenya's capitol, Nairobi, who seem to be immune to the AIDS virus that is killing high-risk co-workers all around them. Most of the women are related. Scientists say it may involve a natural immunity gene that could lead to a vaccine.

Virgin Urgin' Dirge In Scourgin' Purge - The UK's Virgin Net, a Richard Branson "Virgin" subsidiary, pulled a Web game called the "Dunblane Massacre," whereby you could become the Fastest Gun in Dunblane (with a printout badge) by shooting children in what appeared to be a Scottish school yard. The UK still has not recovered from last March's Dunblane incident in which 16 children were killed, resulting in a total UK handgun ban. Virgin also issued a public apology.

Morbidity Limpidity By Liquidity Stupidity - A Tennessee medical examiner says singer Jeff Buckley, who drowned earlier this month attempting to swim in the Mississippi River, was neither drunk nor on drugs. The probable cause of drowning was pegged as wearing heavy boots, which may have hindered his attempts to swim.

The perfect crime was committed last night when thieves broke into Scotland Yard and stole all the toilets. Police say they have nothing to go on.

WE ARE BORN NAKED, WET, AND HUNGRY.
THEN THINGS GET WORSE.

Rockers With Knockers Shock Mockers - The Spice Girls reached the top of the U.S. pop charts with their first album, "Spice."

Aforesaid Ted Forfeited Coveted Coed Head Abed Spread Winifred - A Connecticut man whose golf shot ricocheted off a yardage marker 10 feet away and came back to hit him in the nose has sued the Minnichaug Golf Course for $15,000. His wife is also a plaintiff, claiming mental and emotional anguish due to resulting "curtailment of unspecified family leisure-time activities."

Conclude Nude Brood Who'd Stewed Booboo'd - Ray and Mildred Connett, two longtime American nudist pioneers and promoters, 82, were found dead together in the big hot tub of their Glen Edan, California nudist resort, possibly from overexposure due to their both falling asleep. Police are investigating.

Gored Whore Tour Corps Sore - After word of it leaked, Nevada assemblyman Bob Price had to cancel his "fact-finding-trip" for legislators to the Mustang Ranch brothel in Reno. The media had a field day with it, and Price's office reports it was swamped with requests to join the outing.

Red Tide Eyed In Sea Cowicide - University of Miami scientists say a toxin from Red Tide is what's killing Florida manatees in record numbers. Twelve percent of the manatee population has died just this year.

Fag Nag Sags, Stag Swag Bagged - A stud horse named "Cigar," after a failure at 34 matings, was declared infertile, and an insurance settlement was reached.

Goo Stew Spews New Flu Clue - After a fruitless hunt for decades, scientists have finally located genetic material from the deadly 1918 Spanish flu pandemic, which killed 20 million people. In a young soldier's lung sample preserved at the Armed Forces Pathology Institute, they hope to learn how to combat future flu mutations they say are coming.

Riviera Strip'll Cripple Nipple Ripple - Traditional toplessness on the beach at Cannes has spread to the streets and stores. City officials are now handing out free T-shirts to wandering topless females—mostly tourists.

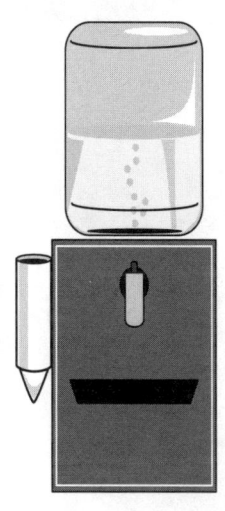

Office Jokes

Some Things To Leave Off Your Résumé...

Qualifications: No education or experience.

Disposed of $2.5 billion in assets.

Personal: Married, 1992 Chevrolet.

My intensity and focus are at inordinately high levels,
and my ability to complete projects on time is unspeakable.

Exposure to German for two years,
but many words are not appropriate for business.

Education: Curses in liberal arts, curses in computer science, curses in accounting.

Instrumental in ruining entire operation for a Midwest chain store.

Proven ability to track down and correct erors.

Personal interests: Donating blood. Fifteen gallons so far.

I have become completely paranoid,
trusting completely nothing and absolutely no one.

References: None. I've left a path of destruction behind me.

Strengths: Ability to meet deadlines while maintaining composer.

Don't take the comments of my former employer too seriously.
They were unappreciative beggars and slave drivers.

My goal is to be a meteorologist. But since I possess no training
in meteorology, I suppose I should try stock brokerage.

I procrastinate, especially when the task is unpleasant.

I am loyal to my employer at all costs. Please feel free
to respond to my résumé on my office voicemail.

The Bigger They Come...

When development engineers go out together on a weekend, they talk football.
When middle managers get together, they talk tennis.
Top management executives discuss golf.

Conclusion:
The higher up in management you are,
the smaller your balls.

Signs You've Had Too Much To Drink At Your Company Picnic...

- You decide to show the boss YOUR version of a "golden parachute."
- Barbara from accounting says, "Slow down, pal. This ain't no Kennedy reunion!"
- People in the Diversity Program don't care much for your Buckwheat impersonation.
- You resurrect that old "Pull My Finger" routine for the folks from the home office.
- You organize an "Armpit Orchestra" to play "Hail to the Chief" when the CEO arrives.
- You offer to teach the boss your procedure for making "Butt Xeroxes."
- You attempt to qualify for the three-legged race — solo.
- You remember "what" to kiss, but forget "whose."
- Evidently a bear's not the only one who can shit in the woods.
- You keep calling your boss "Boo-Boo" and bugging him to help you look for "pic-a-nic" baskets.
- Last words you utter before passing out? "Slide, you fat bastard! Slide!"
- Every time CEO pauses during big speech, you scream, "FREEBIRD!!"
- "But everybody pees in the pool!" (Not from the diving board, my friend).

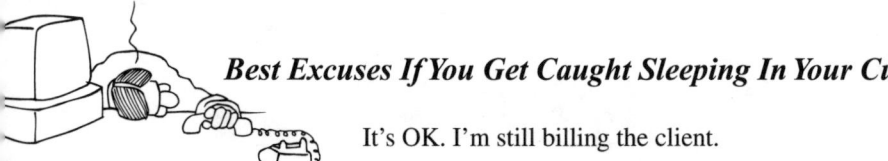

Best Excuses If You Get Caught Sleeping In Your Cubicle...

It's OK. I'm still billing the client.

They told me at the blood bank this might happen.

This is just a 15-minute power-nap like they raved about in the last management course you sent me to.

Whew! Guess I left the top off the liquid paper.

I was meditating on the mission statement and envisioning a new paradigm!

Someone must've put decaf in the wrong pot.

Boy, that cold medicine I took last night just won't wear off!

The coffee machine is broken.

It worked well for Reagan, didn't it?

Ah, the unique and unpredictable ultradian rhythms of the workaholic!

The mailman flipped out and pulled a gun, so I played dead to avoid getting shot.

...and I especially thank you for my excellent boss, Amen!

Actual Excerpts From Employee Evaluations...

He would be out of his depth in a parking lot puddle.

I would not allow this employee to breed.

This young lady has delusions of adequacy.

His men would follow him anywhere, but only out of morbid curiosity.

Since my last report, this employee has reached rock bottom and has started to dig.

This employee should go far—and the sooner he starts, the better.

This employee is depriving a village somewhere of an idiot.

OFFICE MEMO

Quotes From Offices...

Quote from a recent meeting: We're going to continue having these meetings, everyday until I find out why no work is getting done.

Quote from the boss: I didn't say it was your fault. I said I was going to blame it on you.

A motivational sign at work: The beatings will continue until morale improves.

A direct quote from the boss: We passed over a lot of good people to get the ones we hired.

Quote from the boss after overriding the decision of a task force he created to find a solution: I'm sorry if I ever gave you the impression your input would have any effect on my decision for the outcome of this project!

Human Resource Manager to job candidate: I see you've had no computer training. Although that qualifies you for upper management, it means you're underqualified for our entry level positions.

Quote from telephone inquiry: We're only hiring one summer intern this year, and we won't start interviewing candidates for that position until the boss's daughter finishes her summer classes.

My boss frequently gets lost in thought. That's because it's unfamiliar territory.

My boss said to me, "What you see as a glass ceiling, I see as a protective barrier."

My boss needs a surge protector. That way her mouth would be buffered from surprise spikes in her brain.

I thought my boss was a bastard, so I quit to work for myself. My new boss is a bastard, too, but at least I respect him.

He's given automobile accident victims new hope for recovery. He walks, talks, and performs rudimentary tasks, all without the benefit of a SPINE.

Some people climb the ladder of success. My boss walked under it.

I PRETEND TO WORK. THEY PRETEND TO PAY ME.

If You Can't Say Anything Nice...

When you must write a "letter of recommendation" for a fired employee, here are a few suggested phrases:

For the chronically absent: A man like him is hard to find. It seemed his career was just taking off.

For the office drunk: I feel his real talent is wasted here. We generally found him loaded with work to do. Every hour with him was a happy hour.

For an employee with no ambition: He could not care less about the number of hours he had to put in. You would indeed be fortunate to get this person to work for you.

For an employee who is so unproductive that the job is better left unfilled: I can assure you that no person would be better for the job.

For an employee who is not worth further consideration as a job candidate:
I would urge you to waste no time making this candidate an offer of employment.
   or
All in all, I cannot say enough good things about this candidate or recommend him too highly.

For a dishonest employee: Her true ability was deceiving. He's an unbelievable worker.

For a stupid employee: There is nothing you can teach a man like him. I most enthusiastically recommend this candidate with no qualifications whatsoever.

I THOUGHT I WANTED A CAREER.
TURNS OUT I JUST WANTED A PAYCHECK.

This isn't an office.
It's Hell with fluorescent lighting.

I used up all my sick days.
So I called in dead.

A CUBICLE IS JUST A PADDED CELL WITHOUT A DOOR.

Performance Report

Some drink from the fountain of knowledge; he only gargled.

Wheel is turning, but the hamster is dead.

She sets low personal standards and then consistently fails to achieve them.

This employee is not so much of a has-been as a definitely won't-be.

Works well when under constant supervision and cornered like a rat in a trap.

She opens her mouth only to change feet.

Got into the gene pool while the lifeguard wasn't watching.

A room temperature IQ.

A gross ignoramus—144 times worse than an ordinary ignoramus.

A prime candidate for natural deselection.

One-cell organisms outscore him in IQ tests.

Fell out of the family tree.

Gates are down, the lights are flashing, but the train isn't coming.

Has two brains; one lost and the other out looking for it.

He's so dense light bends around him.

If brains were taxed, he'd get a rebate.

If she were any stupider, she'd have to be watered twice a week.

If you stand close enough to her, you can hear the ocean.

One neuron short of a synapse.

Office Procrastinator's Calendar...

NEG	FRI	FRI	FRI	THU	WED	TUE
8	7	6	5	4	3	2
16	15	14	12	11	10	9
23	22	21	20	19	18	17
32	30	28	27	26	25	24
39	38	37	36	35	34	33

1. This is a special calendar for handling rush jobs. All rush jobs were needed yesterday. With this calendar a job or project can be ordered on the 7th and delivered on the 3rd.

2. Many companies set Friday deadlines, so there are three Fridays in every week. This is also beneficial for those persons who are paid on Fridays.

3. There are eight new days added to each month to allow for month-end panic jobs.

4. There is no 1st of the month, thus avoiding late delivery of the previous month's last-minute panic jobs.

5. Monday morning hangovers are abolished, along with nonproductive Saturdays and Sundays.

6. A new day—Negotiation Day—has been introduced, keeping the other days free for uninterrupted panic.

Fired!

A young upwardly-mobile executive was leaving the office one evening when he found the CEO standing in front of a shredder with a piece of paper in his hand.

"Listen," said the CEO, "this is important, and my assistant has left. Can you make this thing work?"

"Certainly," said the young man, flattered that the CEO had asked him for help. He turned the machine on, inserted the paper, and pressed the start button.

"Excellent! Excellent!" said the CEO as his paper disappeared inside the machine.

"I need two copies of that."

Watch Out For The Short Ones...

A man walks up to a woman in his office and tells her that her hair smells nice.

The woman immediately goes into her supervisor's office to tell him that she wants to file a sexual harassment suit.

The supervisor is puzzled at her complaint, "What's wrong with a coworker telling you your hair smells nice?"

The woman replies, "He's a midget."

Paper, Please!

Several years ago we had an intern who was none too swift. One day while typing, he turned to a secretary and said, "I'm almost out of typing paper. What do I do?"

"Just use copier machine paper," she told him. With that, the intern took the last remaining blank piece of paper, put it on the photocopier, and proceeded to make five blank copies.

Why I Fired My Secretary...

Two weeks ago was my 45th birthday, and I wasn't feeling too hot that morning anyway. I went into breakfast, knowing my wife would be pleasant and say "Happy Birthday" and probably have a present for me.

She didn't even say "Good Morning," let alone any "Happy Birthday." I thought, "Well, that's wives for you. The children will remember." The children came to breakfast without saying a word.

When I started for work I was feeling pretty low, even despondent. As I walked into my office, my secretary, Janet, said, "Good Morning, Boss, Happy Birthday." And I felt a little better. Someone had remembered. I worked all morning. About noon Janet knocked on my door and said, "You know, it's such a beautiful day outside and it's your birthday, let's go to lunch, just you and I." I said, "By George, that's the best thing I've heard all day. Let's go."

We went out into the country to a little private place for lunch. We had two martinis and enjoyed the food tremendously. On the way back to the office, she said, "You know, it's such a beautiful day, do we have to go back to the office?" I said, "No, I guess not." She said, "Let's go to my apartment."

After arriving at her apartment, we had another martini and smoked a cigarette, and she said, "Boss, if you don't mind, I think I'll go into the bedroom and slip into something more comfortable." "Sure," I excitedly replied. She went into the bedroom. In about six minutes, she came out—carrying a big birthday cake, followed by my wife, my children, and dozens of our friends.
All were singing Happy Birthday.

... and there on the couch I sat...
... with nothing on but my socks...

Change is inevitable... except from a vending machine.

Philosophy

Things To Ponder...

Why do they lock gas station bathrooms? Are they afraid someone will clean them?

What do you do when you see an endangered animal eating an endangered plant?

If the police arrest a mime, do they tell him he has the right to remain silent?

If a man is standing in the middle of the forest speaking and there is no woman around to hear him, is he still wrong?

If a deaf person swears, does his mother wash his hands with soap?

When sign makers go on strike, is anything written on their signs?

Isn't it a bit unnerving that doctors call what they do "practice?"

Why do they put Braille on the drive-through bank machines?

If a stealth bomber crashes in a forest, will it make a sound?

How do they get the deer to cross at that yellow road sign?

If a turtle doesn't have a shell, is he homeless or naked?

Why do they sterilize the needles for lethal injections?

Where do forest rangers go to "get away from it all?"

Would a fly without wings be called a "walk?"

Why did kamikaze pilots wear helmets?

Why don't sheep shrink when it rains?

Can vegetarians eat animal crackers?

Is there another word for "synonym?"

Still More Things To Ponder...

Good students don't cheat, they verify.

It's a small world, but I wouldn't want to paint it.
Steven Wright

You can't have everything. Where would you put it?
Steven Wright

I went to a restaurant that serves "breakfast at any time." So I ordered French toast during the Renaissance.
Steven Wright

I stayed up all night playing poker with tarot cards.
I got a full house and four people died.
Steven Wright

Right now I'm having amnesia and *deja vu* at the same time.
I think I've forgotten this before.
Steven Wright

It doesn't matter what temperature the room is.
It's always room temperature.
Steven Wright

I don't have any solution, but I certainly admire the problem.
Brilliant

Inside every small problem is a large problem
struggling to get out.

If you think the problem is bad now,
just wait until we've solved it.
Kasspe

Logic is a systematic method of coming
to the wrong conclusion with confidence.
Manly's Maxim

Complex problems have simple,
easy to understand, wrong answers.
Grossman's Misquote

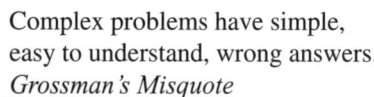

Yet More Things To Ponder...

Only someone who understands something absolutely can explain it so no one else can understand it.
Rudnicki's Nobel Prize Principle

If you don't understand it, it must be intuitively obvious.

I wish there were a knob on the TV to turn up the intelligence. There's a knob called "brightness," but that doesn't work.

If it weren't for the last minute, nothing would get done.

There is no time like the present for postponing what you ought to be doing.

After your hands become coated with grease, your nose will begin to itch.
Lorenz's Law of Mechanical Repair

Any tool, when dropped, will roll into the least accessible corner.
Anthony's Law of the Workshop

> Anything dropped in the bathroom falls into the toilet.
> *Flucard's Corollary*

> The first rule of intelligent tinkering is to save all the parts.
> *Ehrlich*

> If it jams, force it. If it breaks, it needed replacing anyway.
> *Lowery's Law*

> There is no mechanical problem so difficult that it cannot be solved by brute strength and ignorance.
> *William's Law*

> When all else fails, read the instructions.
> *Cann's Axiom*

> When you starve with a tiger, the tiger starves last.
> *Griffin's Thought*

> The other line moves faster.
> *Ettore's Observation*

> Proofreading is almost foolproof after publication.

More Or Less Useful Thoughts...

If at first you don't succeed, destroy all evidence that you ever tried.

A conclusion is the place where you got tired of thinking.

Experience is something you don't get until after you need it.

For every action there is an equal and opposite criticism.

He who hesitates is probably right.

Never do card tricks for your poker buddies.

No one is listening until you make a mistake.

Success always occurs in private; failure happens in full view.

The hardness of the butter is proportional to the softness of the bread.

To succeed in politics, it is often necessary to rise above your principles.

Two wrongs are only the beginning.

Monday is an awful way to spend one seventh of your life.

Plan to be spontaneous tomorrow.

Better living through denial.

A clear conscience is usually the sign of a bad memory.

Don't sweat petty things... or pet sweaty things.

A fool and his money are soon partying.

Money can't buy love. But it CAN rent a very close imitation.

Always try to be modest. And be damn proud of it!

The sooner you fall behind, the more time you'll have to catch up.

Even More Or Less Useful Thoughts...

If you think nobody cares about you, try missing a couple of payments.

How many of you believe in telekinesis? Raise my hands.

Attempt to get a new car for your spouse—it'll be a great trade!

Drugs may lead nowhere, but at least you'll travel the scenic route.

I'd kill for a Nobel Peace Prize.

Everybody repeat after me, "We are all individuals."

Death to all fanatics!

Guests who kill talk show hosts—on the last Geraldo.

Chastity is curable, if detected early.

If all else fails, throw up.

Love may be blind, but marriage is a real eyeopener.

Hell hath no fury like the lawyer of a woman scorned.

Bills travel through the mail at twice the speed of checks.

Hard work pays off in the future. Laziness pays off now.

Eagles may soar, but weasels aren't sucked into jet engines.

Borrow money from pessimists. They don't expect it back.

Half the people you know are below average.

Of all statistics, 42.7 percent are made up on the spot.

A conscience is what hurts when all your other parts feel so good.

And Thus It Was Written

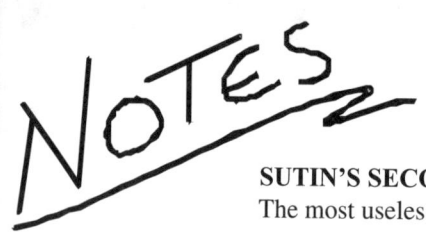

On Laws And Some Order...

SUTIN'S SECOND LAW: The most useless computer tasks are the most fun to do.

HIGDON'S LAW: Good judgment comes from experience. Experience comes from bad judgment.

CHURCHILL'S COMMENTARY ON MAN: Man will occasionally stumble over the truth, but most of the time he will pick himself up and continue.

FOX ON LEVELOLOGY: What will get you promoted on one level will get you killed on another.

EDD'S LAW OF RADIOLOGY: The colder the x-ray table, the more of your body you will be required to place on it.

MURPHY'S LAW OF THERMODYNAMICS: Things get worse under pressure.

COURTOIS' RULE: If people listened to themselves more often, they would talk less.

FOX ON PROBLEMATICS: Even though the problem goes away, the people working to solve it do not.

JACOBSON'S LAW: The less work an organization produces, the more frequently it reorganizes.

GRANDPA CHARNOCK'S LAW: You never really learn to swear until you learn to drive.

THE PITFALLS OF GENIUS: No boss will keep an employee who is right all the time.

PHILLIPS' LAW: Four-wheel drive just means getting stuck in more inaccessible places.

RUCKERT'S LAW: There is nothing so small it can't be blown out of proportion.

GOURD'S AXIOM: A meeting is an event at which the minutes are kept while the hours lost.

CAMPBELL'S LAW OF AUTOMOTIVE REPAIR: If you can get to the faulty part, you don't have the tool to get it off.

STEINBACH'S GUIDELINE FOR SYSTEMS PROGRAMMING: Never test for an error condition you don't know how to handle.

BRINTNALL'S SECOND LAW: If you are given two contradictory orders, obey them both.

LAW OF POLITICAL MACHINERY: When no viable candidate exists, someone will nominate a Kennedy.

SOUDER'S LAW: Repetition does not establish validity.

HECHT'S FOURTH LAW: There's no time like the present for postponing what you don't want to do.

LAW OF INSTITUTIONS: The opulence of the front office decor varies inversely with the fundamental solvency of the firm.

LOFTUS' THEORY ON PERSONNEL RECRUITMENT: Faraway talent always seems better than home-developed talent.

LAUNEGAYER'S OBSERVATION: Asking dumb questions is easier than correcting dumb mistakes.

GROSSMAN'S MISQUOTE OF H.L. MENCKEN: Complex problems have simple, easy-to-understand wrong answers.

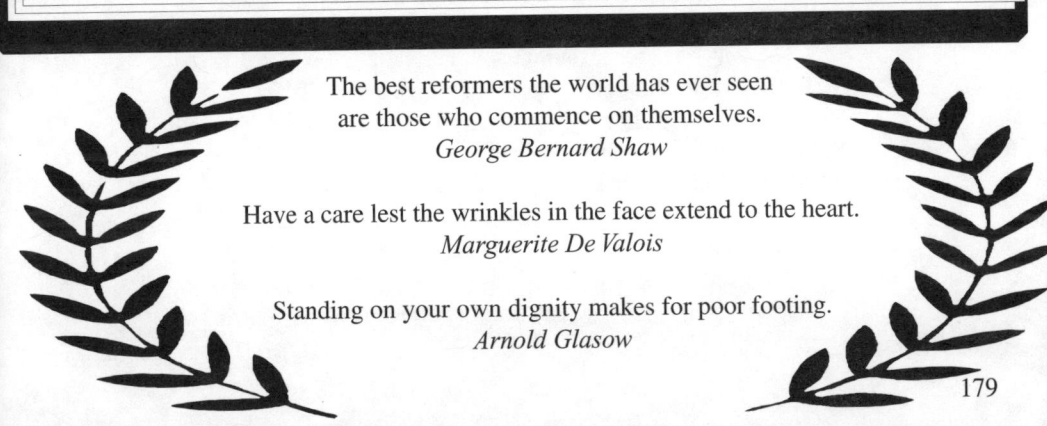

The best reformers the world has ever seen
are those who commence on themselves.
George Bernard Shaw

Have a care lest the wrinkles in the face extend to the heart.
Marguerite De Valois

Standing on your own dignity makes for poor footing.
Arnold Glasow

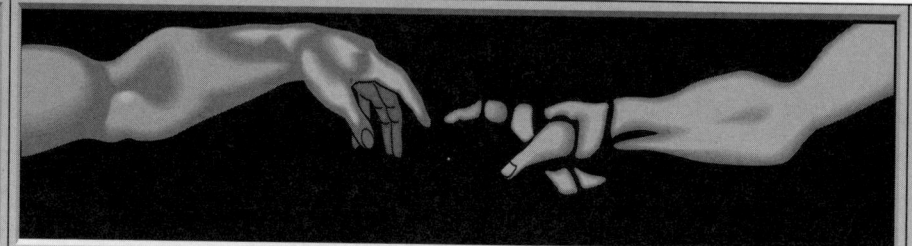

Some Creative Thoughts To Get You Through The Day...

Incontinence Hotline. Can you hold, please?
Lysdexia—a peech imspediment we live to learn with.
If only women came with pull-down menus and on-line help.
Would the Standing Committee please sit down?
OK, OK, I take it back! Unscrew you!
The difference between avoiding taxes and evading taxes is 10 years.
Circular Definition: see Definition, Circular.
A.A.A.A.A.—An organization for drunks who drive.
It said "Insert disk #3," but only two will fit.
For a REAL sponge cake, BORROW all the ingredients.
Bacon & eggs—Hens are involved but pigs are committed.
Which is the nonsmoking lifeboat?
Originality is the art of concealing your sources.
Just fill out one simple form to win an IRS audit!
Paper clips are the larval stage of coat hangers.
Contents may have settled out of court.
If idiots could fly, this place would be an airport.
A seminar on Time Travel will be held two weeks ago.
Democracy—four wolves and a lamb voting on lunch.
Would you trust a POLITICIAN to run the country?
Improve mail delivery. Mail the posties their pay!!
Thank you for holding your breath while I smoke.
Treat each day as your last. One day you will be right.
Old is always 15 years older than I am.
I am the root of some evil. Send some money.
The buck doesn't even slow down here!
Don't assume malice for what can explained by stupidity.
If you think talk is cheap, try hiring a lawyer.
Oh, no! Not ANOTHER learning experience!
The only cure for insomnia is to get more sleep.
Don't question authority. It doesn't have a clue!!!!!
Advice is free. The right answer will cost plenty.
Stupidity does not qualify as a handicap. Park elsewhere!
Multitasking = screwing up several things at once.
Looking for a helping hand? There's one on your arm.
Don't take life too seriously. It's not permanent.
Don't insult the alligator till after you cross the river.
||||||////// __ __ __ __ __ The domino effect at work.

Some Other Creative Thoughts To Get You Through The Day...

Sarcasm is just one more service we offer.
Nothing's impossible for those who don't have to do it.
History is a set of lies agreed on by the victors.
After four decimal places, nobody cares.
One good turn gets all the blankets.
Almost all loan officers have artificial hearts.
Two can live as cheaply as one, for half as long.
War never decides who's right, only who's left.
A job is nice, but it interferes with my life.
Don't worry. The answer's in the back of the book.
A crowded elevator smells different to a midget.
Support the right to arm bears.
We do precision guesswork.
My life has a superb cast, but I can't figure out the plot.
Don't let school interfere with your education.
"Oh, what a tangled web we weave": Hair Club for Men.
Shin: A device for finding furniture in the dark.
Depression is merely anger without enthusiasm.
I'm not cheap, but I am on special this week.
I drive way too fast to worry about cholesterol.
Mind like a steel trap: Rusty and illegal in 37 states.
Support bacteria. They're the only culture some people have.
Televangelists: The pro wrestlers of religion.
The only substitute for good manners is fast reflexes.
When everything's coming your way, you're in the wrong lane.
If everything is going well, obviously you have overlooked something.
Many people quit looking for work when they find a job.
When I'm not in my right mind, my left mind gets pretty crowded.
What happens if you get scared half to death twice?
How do you tell when you run out of invisible ink?
Laughing stock: Cattle with a sense of humor.
Why do psychics have to ask you for your name?
Black holes are where God divided by zero.
Those who live by the sword get shot by those who don't.
And your crybaby whiny-assed opinion would be...?
Nothing is foolproof to a sufficiently talented fool.
If you can't be kind, at least have the decency to be vague.
Clones are people two.
Earn cash in your spare time—blackmail your friends.

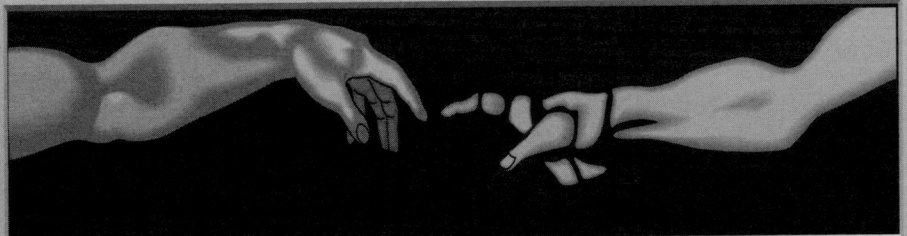

Grow your own dope. Plant a politician.

Quotes From Dan Quayle

As Dave Barry says, "Folks, I am not making this up." In fact, ex-Vice President J. Danforth Quayle actually did say these:

If we don't succeed, we run the risk of failure.

Welcome to President Bush, Mrs. Bush, and my fellow astronauts.
At the Apollo 11 anniversary celebration.

Mars is essentially in the same orbit... Mars is somewhat the same distance from the sun, which is very important. We have seen pictures where there are canals, we believe, and water. If there is water, that means there is oxygen. If oxygen, that means we can breathe.

I was recently on a tour of Latin America, and the only regret I have was that I didn't study Latin harder in school so I could converse with those people.

What a waste it is to lose one's mind. Or not to have a mind is being very wasteful. How true that is.
Quayle during a fund-raising event for the United Negro College Fund, which was using "A mind is a terrible thing to waste" as its slogan.

The Holocaust was an obscene period in our nation's history. I mean in this century's history. But we all lived in this century. I didn't live in this century.

I believe we are on an irreversible trend toward more freedom and democracy—but that could change.

One word sums up probably the responsibility of any vice president, and that one word is, "to be prepared."

May our nation continue to be the beakon (sic) of hope to the world.
From the Quayles' 1989 Christmas card (but not a beacon of literacy however.)

We don't want to go back to tomorrow. We want to go forward.

Still More Nuggets Of Wisdom From Dan Quayle...

The future will be better tomorrow.

Republicans understand the importance of bondage between a mother and child.

Verbosity leads to unclear, inarticulate things.

I support efforts to limit the terms of members of congress, especially members of the House and members of the Senate.

We have a firm commitment to NATO. We are a part of NATO. We have a firm commitment to Europe. We are a part of Europe.

I have made good judgements in the past. I have made good judgements in the future.

People that are really weird can get into sensitive positions and have a tremendous impact on history.

I stand by all the misstatements that I've made.

[It's] time for the human race to enter the Solar System.

It isn't pollution that's harming the environment. It's the impurities in our air and water that are doing it.

We're all capable of mistakes, but I do not care to enlighten you on the mistakes we may or may not have made.

When I have been asked during these last weeks who caused the riots and killing in L.A., my answer has been direct and simple. Who is to blame for the riots? The rioters are to blame. Who is to blame for the killings? The killers are to blame.

Still More Misstatement Gems From Everyone's Favorite, Dan Quayle...

I am not part of the problem. I am a Republican.

I love California. I practically grew up in Phoenix.

Illegitimacy is something we should
talk about in terms of not having it.

A low voter turnout is an indication of fewer people going to the polls.

Murphy Brown is doing better than I am. At least she knows she has a job next year.

For NASA, space is still a high priority.

We are ready for any unforeseen event that may or may not occur.

Quite frankly, teachers are the only profession that teach our children.

The American people would not want to know
of any misquotes that Dan Quayle may or may not make.

Public speaking is very easy.
Dan Quayle

Keep honking... I'm reloading.

Rednecks & Cowboys

There Are Some Things A Cowboy Just Won't Do...

Two cowboys are out in the woods rounding up cattle. They stop to cook some lunch when Tex decides he needs to pee.

He ambles off a short distance and starts to do his business, peeing over a fallen log. On the log, a rattlesnake has been sunning itself and, of course, doesn't take kindly to the bath he got.

So the snake ups and bites the cowboy on his "Johnson." Now Tex doesn't like being bitten there, so he starts to scream bloody murder. His friend Rex comes running to see what the commotion is all about.

Tex quickly tells Rex what had happened. "What medicine can I take?" asks Tex. "I don't know, but I do remember hearing that you should stay still and be calm. I'll ride to town to get the Doc and find out what to do."

So Rex rides to town, not sparing the horse. Pulling up to the doctor's office in a cloud of dust, he runs in and tells the Doc a rattler has bitten Tex.

"What needs to be done, Doc? Can you come out and take care of Tex?"

"Mrs. Ryan is about to have her baby, so I can't come. But here's what to do. Make a cut with this scalpel in the shape of an "X" at the fang mark. Then you have to suck out all the poison."

"Say, Doc, what happens if this ain't done?" asks Rex.

"It's very likely Rex will die." says the Doc.

Rex rides back a bit slower and finds Tex lying in the shade alive, but sinking fast.

"WHAT DID THE DOC SAY?" Tex gasps.

Looking distraught, Rex replies, "He said you're gonna die, ol' boy."

Etiquette Tips For Rednecks...

Personal Hygiene

Unlike clothes and shoes, a toothbrush should never be a hand-me-down.

While ears need to be cleaned regularly, this is a job that should be done in private using one's OWN truck keys.

Proper use of toiletries can forestall bathing for several days. However, if you live alone, deodorant is a waste of good money.

Dirt and grease under the fingernails is a social no-no, as they tend to detract from a woman's jewelry and alter the tastes of finger foods.

Plucking unwanted nose hair is time-consuming work. A cigarette lighter and a small tolerance for pain can accomplish the same goal and save hours. It's a good idea to keep a bucket of water handy when using this method.

Dining Out

If drinking directly from the bottle, always hold it with your fingers covering the label.

Remember to leave a generous tip for good service. After all, their mobile homes cost just as much as yours.

When decanting wine, make sure you tilt the paper cup and pour slowly so as not to "bruise" the fruit of the vine.

Entertaining In Your Home

Do not allow the dog to eat at the table—no matter how good his manners.

Be considerate of your guests. Point out in advance where the injury-threatening springs are poking through the sofa.

If your dog falls in love with a guest's leg, have the decency to leave them alone for a few minutes.

A centerpiece for the table should never be anything prepared by a taxidermist.

Uh, Oh, Tonto!

The Lone Ranger and Tonto have been riding down the trail when they decide to rest. Tonto places his ear to the ground to listen.
"Buffalo come," reports Tonto.
"How can you tell, Tonto?" asks the Lone Ranger.

"Face sticky, smell."

Things You'll Hear Only In The South...

Exclamations:
Well knock me down and steal muh teeth!
Well, butter my butt and call me a biscuit.

Threats:
I'll slap you so hard, your clothes will be outta style.
This'll jar your preserves.

Good Things/Compliments:
Cute as a sackful of puppies.
If things get any better, I may have to hire someone to help me enjoy it.

The Weather:
It's so dry, the trees are bribing the dogs.
It's been hotter'n a goat's butt in a pepper patch.

Descriptions:
When something is bad, you say "That ain't no count."
If something is hard to do, it's "Like trying to herd cats."
He ran "Like his feet was on fire and his ass was catchin."
A hectic schedule keeps you "Busier than a cat covering crap on a marble floor."

Insults:
She's uglier than homemade soap.
He fell out of the ugly tree and hit every branch on the way down.
Uglier than a lard bucket full of armpits.
Any insulting statement is always followed by
"Bless his/her heart"

Smile When You Fold That, Partner...

A tall weatherworn cowboy walked into the saloon and ordered a beer. The regulars quietly observed the drifter through half-closed eyelids. No one spoke, but they all noticed that the stranger's hat was made of brown wrapping paper. Less obvious was the fact that his shirt and vest were also made of paper. As were his chaps, pants, and even his boots, including the paper spurs. Truth be told, even the saddle, blanket, and bridle on his horse were made entirely of paper.

Of course he was soon arrested for rustling...

NEVER SQUAT WITH YOUR SPURS ON!

A Real Cowboy...

An old cowboy dressed to kill with cowboy shirt, hat, jeans, spurs, and chaps went to a bar and ordered a drink. As he sat there sipping his whiskey, a young lady sat down next to him. After she ordered her drink she turned to the cowboy and asked him, "Are you a real cowboy?"

To which he replied, "Well, I've spent my whole life on the ranch, herding cows, breaking horses, mending fences, I guess I am."

After a short while he asked her what she was. She replied, "I've never been on a ranch, so I'm not a cowboy, but I am a lesbian. I spend my whole day thinking about women. As soon as I get up in the morning, I think of women. When I eat, shower, watch TV, everything seems to make me think of women."

A short while after she left, the cowboy ordered another drink. A couple sat down next to him, and the woman asked, "Are you a real cowboy?"

"I always thought I was, Ma'am, but I just found out I'm a lesbian."

Yankees Beware...

A Texan, a New Yorker, and a Massachusetts resident were drinking their favorite beverage in a bar. The Texan drained his glass of tequila, threw the half full bottle up in the air, drew and fired his pistol, shattering the bottle. The other two were shocked at his ruining perfectly good tequila. The Texan however, simply drew himself up and announced: "Where I come from, we have plenty of tequila."

The New Yorker, not to be outdone, drained his glass of wine, threw the wine bottle into the air, and drew and fired his pistol, also shattering his bottle. Looking over at the other two with an air of superiority, he announced, "Where I come from, we have plenty of fine wine as well as the best of everything else in life!"

The Massachusetts resident drained his bottle of Sam Adam's Ale, threw it up in the air, drew his pistol, and shot the New Yorker dead. He then caught the bottle on the way down and showed it to the Texan: "Where I come from," he said slowly, "we recycle these—but we have plenty of New Yorkers already."

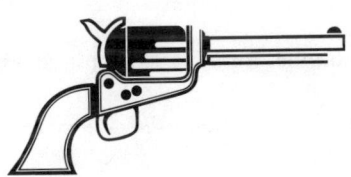

Choking...

Two Texans were drinking at the end of a bar when a young lady seated a few stools up choked on a piece of hamburger. As she started turning blue, one Texan said to the other "That there gal is having a bad time!" The other agreed, "Think we should go help?" "You bet," said the first, and with that he ran over and said, "Can you breathe???" She shook her head "No." He said, "Can you speak???" Again she shook her head.

With that he pulled up her skirt and licked her on the butt. So shocked was the young woman that she coughed up the obstruction and began to breathe with great relief. Back to his friend, the Texan said, "Funny how that hind-lick maneuver always works!"

Hickbonics...

Heidi - *(noun)* - Greeting.

Hire Yew - Complete sentence. Remainder of greeting.
>Usage: Heidi, hire yew?

Bard - *(verb)* - Past tense of the infinitive "to borrow."
>Usage: My brother bard my pickup truck.

Jawjuh - *(noun)* - The state north of Florida. Capital is Lanner.
>Usage: My brother from Jawjuh bard my pickup truck.

Bammer - *(noun)* - The state west of Jawjuh. Capital is Berminhayum.
>Usage: A Bammer tornader left $20 million in improvements.

Munts - *(noun)* - A calendar division.
>Usage: My brother bard my truck, and I ain't herd from him in munts.

Bare - *(noun)* - An alcoholic beverage made of barley, hops, and yeast.
>Usage: Ah thank ah'll have a bare.

Thank - *(verb)* - Ability to cognitively process.
>Usage: Ah thank ah'll have a bare.

All - *(noun)* - A petroleum-based lubricant.
>Usage: I sure hope my brother from Jawjuh puts all in my pickup truck.

Far - *(noun)* - A conflagration.
>Usage: If my brother don't change the all, my pickup's gonna catch far.

Tar - *(noun)* - A rubber wheel.
>Usage: Gee, I hope my brother from Jawjuh don't git a flat tar in my pickup.

Tire - *(noun)* - A tall monument.
>Usage: Lord willin' and the creek don't rise, I hope to see that Eiffel Tire.

Farn - *(adjective)* - Not domestic.
>Usage: I cuddint unnerstand a wurd he sed...must be farn.

Bob War - *(noun)* - A sharp, twisted cable.
>Usage: Boy, stay away from that bob war fence.

Jew Here - *(noun)* and *(verb)* contraction.
>Usage: Jew here my brother got a job with that bob war fence cump'ny?

Retard - *(verb)* - To stop working.
>Usage: My grampaw retard at age 65.

Did - *(adjective)* - Not alive.
>Usage: He's did, Jim.

Ear - *(noun)* - A colorless, odorless gas; *i.e.* Oxygen.
>Usage: He cain't breathe. Give 'im some ear!

Haze - a contraction.
>Usage: Is Bubba smart? Nah. Haze ignert.

Seed - *(verb)* - past tense of "to see."

View - contraction: *(verb)* and *(pronoun)*.
>Usage: I ain't never seed New York City... view?

Gubmint - *(noun)* - A bureaucratic institution.
>Usage: Them gubmint boys shore is ignert.

How To Tell If A Redneck Is Working At The Office Computer...

The mouse is referred to as a "critter."
The keyboard is camouflaged.
There is a Skoal can in the CD-ROM drive.
The password is "bubba."
The numeric keypad only goes up to six.
"Winders 95" has a Dale Earnhardt sticker on it.
Outgoing faxes are covered with beer stains.
The printer goes really slow since Bubba don't read too fast.
Dodge truck parts are installed in the extra RAM slots.
The menus all have Budweiser, Black Label, and Old Milwaukee options.
The monitor is up on blocks.
Seven blue-tick hounds loll under the desk.
Deer jerky is crammed into the desk drawer.
The screen-saver has a Ned Beatty picture and plays "Dueling Banjos."
The six front keys have rotted out.
The operator wears John Deere pocket protectors.

Too Dumb For Takeout...

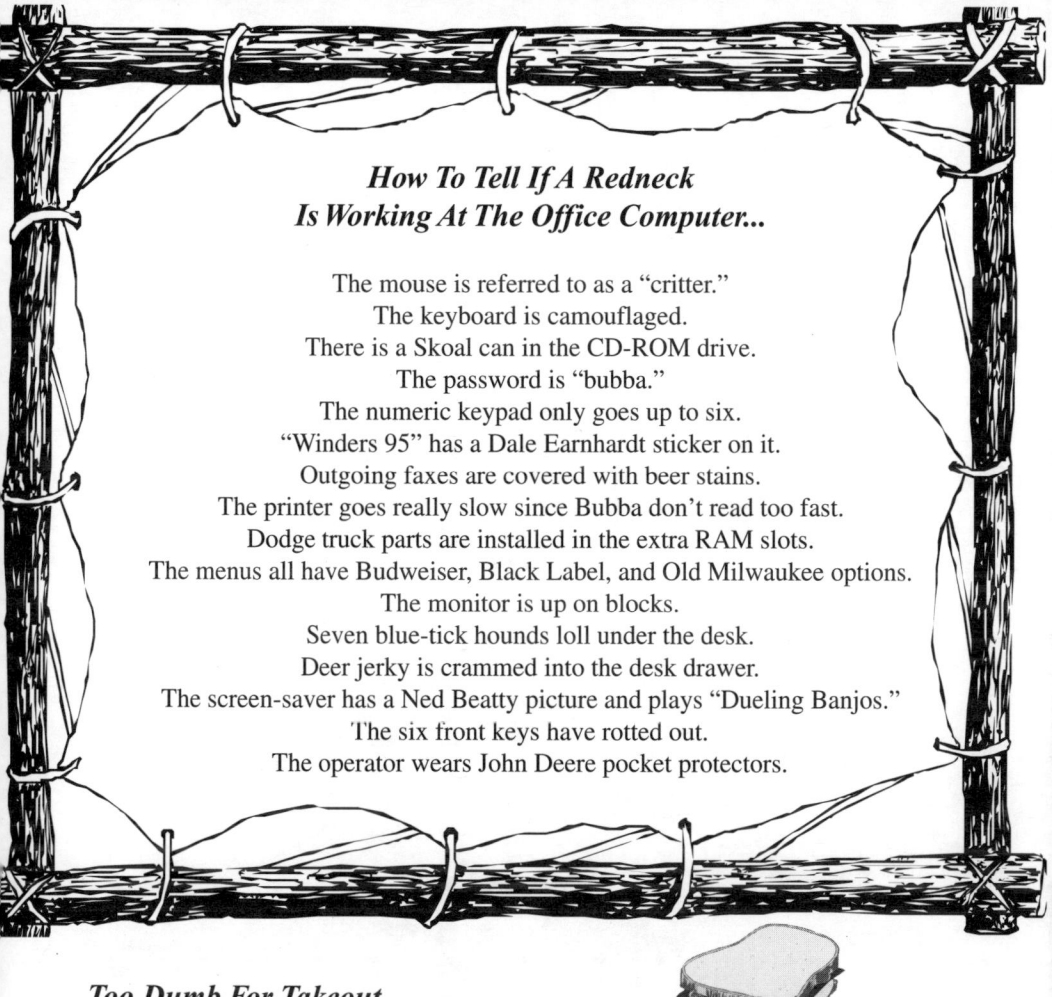

An Irishman, a Mexican, and a redneck were working on scaffolding on the 20th floor of a new building. At their lunch break the Irishman said, "Corned beef and cabbage! If I get corned beef and cabbage one more time, I'm going to jump off this building."

The Mexican opened his lunch box, "Burritos again! If I get burritos one more time, I'm going to jump too." The redneck opened his lunch and said, "Baloney again. If I get a baloney sandwich one more time, I'm jumping too." The next day the Irishman opened his lunch box, saw corned beef and cabbage, and jumped to his death. The Mexican opened his lunch, saw a burrito, and leaped too. The redneck opened his lunch, found the bologna, and followed them to his death.

At the funeral the Irishman's wife cried, "If I'd known how tired he was of corned beef and cabbage, I never would have given it to him again!" The Mexican's wife cried, "I could have given him tacos or enchiladas! I didn't realize he hated burritos so much." Everyone turned to the redneck's wife. "Hey, don't look at me," she said. "He made his own lunch."

Relationships

Think Before You Speak...

A wife asks her husband, "Honey, if I died, would you remarry?"

"After a considerable period of grieving, I guess I would. We all need companionship."

"If I died and you remarried," the wife asks, "would she live in this house?"

"We've spent a lot of money getting this house just the way we want it. I'm not going to get rid of my house. I guess she would."

"If I died and you remarried and she lived in this house," the wife asks, "would she sleep in our bed?"

"Well, the bed is brand new, and it cost us $2,000. It's going to last a long time, so I guess she would."

"If I died and you remarried and she lived in this house and slept in our bed, would she use my golf clubs?"

"Oh, no," the husband replies. "She's left-handed."

Say Again...

A man and his wife started out in their car after a quarrel. She sat in the back seat and continued to berate him for his faults. In her excitement she pounded on the car door, and it flew open. Several blocks later one of their neighbors flagged the man down.

"Your wife fell out of the car back there," he said. The man looked over at the back seat.

"Thank goodness!" he said. "I thought I'd lost my hearing."

Convict Plan...

An escaped convict broke into a house and tied up the young couple he found sleeping in the bedroom.

As soon as the husband had a chance, he turned to his voluptuous young wife, bound up on the bed in a skimpy nightgown, and whispered, "Honey, this guy hasn't seen a woman in years. Just cooperate with anything he wants. If he wants to have sex with you, go along with it and pretend you like it. Our lives may depend on it."

"Dear," the wife hissed, spitting out her gag, "I'm so relieved you feel that way, because he just told me he thinks you're really cute!"

Did the aliens forget to remove your anal probe?

MY WIFE RAN OFF WITH MY BEST FRIEND, AND I SURE DO MISS HIM.

Two Can Play...

A woman is in bed with her lover, who also happens to be her husband's best friend. They have sex for several hours. Afterwards, while they're resting, the phone rings. Since they're in the woman's house, she picks up the receiver. Her lover looks over and listens, only hearing her side of the conversation.

(She's speaking in a cheery voice.) "Hello? Oh, hi. I'm so glad you've called. Really? That's wonderful. I'm happy for you. That sounds terrific. Great! Thanks. OK. Bye bye."

After she hangs up the telephone, her lover asks, "Who was that?"

"Oh," she replies, "that was my husband telling me all about the wonderful time he was having on his fishing trip with you."

How To Make Friends...

She was wearing a very tight skirt. When the Fifth Avenue bus stopped, she tried to board but found she couldn't lift her leg high enough. She reached back to unzip her zipper. It didn't seem to do any good, so she reached back and unzipped again. Suddenly the man behind her lifted her up and put her on the top step.

"How dare you?" she demanded.

"Well, lady," he said, "by the time you unzipped my fly for the second time, I thought we were good friends."

The Difference Between Men And Women...

A man is driving up a steep narrow mountain road. A woman is driving down the same road in the opposite direction.

As they pass each other, the woman leans out the window and yells, "PIG!!"

The man immediately leans out his window and responds "BITCH!!!"

They continue their separate ways. As the man rounds the next corner, he drives full speed into a pig crossing the road.

Pass Me The 5-Iron...

The room was full of pregnant women and their partners. The Lamaze class was in full swing. The instructor was teaching the women how to breathe properly and informing the men how to give the necessary assurances at this stage of the birth process.

The teacher announced, "Ladies, exercise is good for you. Walking is especially beneficial. And, gentlemen, it wouldn't hurt you to take the time to go walking with your partner!" The room, half occupied by men, got really quiet.

Finally, a man in the middle of the group raised his hand. "Yes?" asked the teacher. "While we walk, is it all right if she carries my golf bag?"

197

Why Abby Is America's Most Popular Advice-Giver...

Dear Abby:
I have a man I can't trust.
He cheats on me so much I'm not even sure this baby I'm carrying is his.

Dear Abby:
I'm a 23-year-old liberated woman who has been on the pill for two years. It's getting expensive, and I think my boyfriend should share half the cost. But I don't know him well enough to discuss money with him.

Dear Abby:
I suspected that my husband had been fooling around. When I confronted him with the evidence, he denied everything and said it would never happen again.

Dear Abby:
I was married to Bill for three months, and I didn't know he drank
until one night he came home sober.

Dear Abby:
My mother is mean and short-tempered.
I think she is going through her mental pause.

Dear Abby:
My boyfriend is going to be 20 years old next month. I'd like to give him something nice for his birthday. What do you think he'd like? Signed, Carol

A: Dear Carol: Never mind what he'd like. Give him a tie.

Dear Abby:
I have always wanted to have my family history traced. But I can't afford to spend a lot of money to do it. Any suggestions? Signed, Sam.

A: Dear Sam: Yes. Run for public office.

Dear Abby:
I am 44 years old and would like to meet a man
my age with no bad habits. Signed, Rose.

A: Dear Rose: So would I.

Dear Abby:
What's the difference between a wife and a mistress? Signed, Bess.

A: Dear Bess: Night and day.

Come As You Are...

An African-American husband and wife had been invited to a Halloween party. The husband asked his wife to go to the store to rent costumes for them. When he came home that night, he found his wife had laid out a Superman costume. The husband yelled, "What are you thinking? Have you ever heard of a black Superman! Take this back and get me something I can wear."

The next day his unhappy wife took it back. When the husband came home, he found a Batman costume. Again he yelled at her, "What are you doing? Have you ever heard of a black Batman? Take this back and get me something I can wear to the party." By this time, the wife was irate. Next morning she went shopping again.

When the husband came home that night, laid out on the bed were five items. First were three white buttons; then a white belt; finally a wooden 2x4. The husband yelled at the wife, "What the hell are these for?"

The wife yelled back. "You can take your clothes off, stick these three white buttons down your front, and go as a domino. If you don't like that, you can put on the belt and go as a Oreo cookie. And if you don't like that, you can stick the 2x4 up your black ass and go as a fudgesicle."

Check Your Calendar...

"I bet you don't know what day this is," said the wife to her husband as he made his way out the front door.

The husband was perplexed but was always a quick thinker. "Of course I do, my dear. How could I forget!?" With that, he turned and rushed to catch the bus for work.

At 10 a.m. the doorbell rang, and when the woman opened the door, she was handed a box containing a dozen long-stemmed red roses. At 1 p.m. a foil-wrapped two-pound box of her favorite chocolates arrived. Later a boutique delivered a designer dress. The woman couldn't wait for her husband to come home.

The husband was smug when he returned from work, satisfied that he had recovered what could have been a very bad situation.

His wife was indeed surprised. "First the flowers, then the chocolates, and then the dress!" she exclaimed, "I've never had a more wonderful Groundhog Day in my life!"

The Airplane Trip To Heaven...

A man walks onto an airplane and takes his seat. He looks up and notices the most beautiful woman he has ever seen boarding the plane. Soon he realizes that she is walking down the aisle toward him. He is so nervous. When she takes the seat right next to him, he is anxious to begin a conversation with her.

He asks, "Where are you flying to today?" She responds, "To the annual Nymphomaniac Convention in Chicago." He is CRAZED with excitement! Here is a gorgeous woman sitting next to him, and she's going to a meeting of nymphomaniacs!!!!

"And what do you do at this meeting?" he asks. "Well," she says, "we try to expose and eliminate some of the popular myths about sexuality."

"And what myths are those?" he goes on desperately. She explains, "Well, one popular myth is that African-American men are the most physically endowed, when in fact, it is the Native-American who have the largest. Also, it is widely believed that Frenchman are the best lovers, when actually it is Jewish males who make the best lovers."

"Very interesting," the man responds. Suddenly, the woman becomes very embarrassed and blushes. "I'm sorry," she says, "I just feel so awkward discussing this with you when I don't even know you! What's your name?"

The man extends his hand and replies, "Tonto. Tonto Goldstein."

If you want your wife to pay strict attention to every word you say, talk in your sleep.

The Lottery...

This man runs home and bursts in yelling, "Pack your bags, Honey. I just won the lottery!"

She says, "Great! Should I pack for the beach or the mountains?"

He replies, "I don't care. Just get the hell out!"

Things You'll Never Hear A Man Say...

Here, Honey, you use the remote.

You know, I'd like to see her again, but her breasts are just too big.

Ooh, Antonio Banderas AND Brad Pitt? That's one movie I've gotta see!

While I'm up, may I get you anything?

Sex isn't that important. Sometimes I just want to be held.

Aww, forget Monday night football. Let's watch *Melrose Place*.

Here, let me hold your purse while you try that on.

We never talk anymore.

Things You'll Never Hear A Woman Say...

Honey, don't stop for directions.
I'm sure you'll be able to figure out how to get there.

Can our relationship get a little more physical? I'm tired of being "just friends."

I don't care if it's on sale, $300 is way too much for a designer dress.

Let's not talk to each other tonight. I'd rather watch TV.

Ohhhhhh, this diamond is wayyyyyyyyy tooooooo big!

Honey, does this outfit make my butt look too small?

What do you mean today's our anniversary?

Hey, pull my finger!

Religious Jokes

An Easy Mistake...

The old pope dies and naturally, he goes to Heaven. He's met by the reception committee, and after a whirlwind tour of the establishment, he's told that he can enjoy any of the myriad recreations available. He decides he wants to read all of the ancient original texts of the Holy Scriptures and he spends the next eon or so learning the various languages.

After becoming a linguistic master, the pope sits down in the library and begins to pore over every known version of the Bible, working back from the most recent "easy reading" to several original scripts. For ages his scholarly studies keep him quietly absorbed until one day all of a sudden there comes an almighty scream from the library.

The angels come running to him, only to find the pope huddled in a chair, crying to himself and muttering despairingly, "An 'R'! They left out the 'R'."

God takes him aside, offers him comfort, and inquires what has distressed him. After collecting his wits, the pope sobs again, "It's the letter 'R'! It's the 'R.'"

The word was supposed to be
    CELEBRATE!"

Pity The Pope...

A drunk got on a bus one day and sat down next to a priest. The drunk's shirt was stained, his face was full of lipstick, and he had half a bottle of wine in his pocket. Opening his paper and reading, he asked the priest, "Father, what causes arthritis?"

"It's caused by loose living, being with cheap women, and drinking too much alcohol." "Well I'll be damned," the drunk muttered and returned to reading his paper.

The priest, thinking about what he said, turned to the man and apologized. "I'm sorry, I didn't mean to come on so strong. How long have you had arthritis?" "I don't, Father, I was just reading in the paper that the pope has it."

New Route...

Two Italian nuns are riding their rickety old bikes down the back streets of Rome one late afternoon. As day turns to dusk, the increasing darkness starts making one of the nuns a little nervous. She leans over to the other and says, "You know, I've never come this way before." The other nun says, "It's the cobblestones."

Adam & Eve...

Adam was walking around the Garden of Eden feeling very lonely, so God asked Adam, "What is wrong?"

Adam said he didn't have anyone to talk to. God said he was going to give him a companion and it would be a woman. He said, "This person will cook for you and wash your clothes. She will always agree with every decision you make. She will bear you children and never ask you to get up in the middle of the night to take care of them. She will not nag you. In fact, when you've had a disagreement, she will always be the first to admit she was wrong. She will never have a headache, and she will freely give you love and compassion whenever you need it.

Adam asked God, "What would a woman like this cost?"
God said, "An arm and a leg."
Adam said "What can I get for a just a rib?"

The rest is history.

Sisters Of Mercy...

A man is driving down a deserted stretch of highway in Nevada when he notices a sign out of the corner of his eye. It reads:

SISTERS OF MERCY HOUSE OF PROSTITUTION - 10 MILES

He thinks it was just a figment of his imagination and drives on without a second thought. When he sees another sign, he realizes that these signs are for real. When he drives past a third sign saying

SISTERS OF MERCY HOUSE OF PROSTITUTION - NEXT RIGHT

his curiosity gets the best of him and he pulls into the drive. On the far side of the parking lot is a somber stone building with a small sign next to the door reading

SISTERS OF MERCY

He climbs the steps and rings the bell. The door is answered by a nun who asks, "What may we do for you, my son?" He answers, "I saw your signs along the highway." "Very well, my son. Please follow me."

She leads him through many winding passages until he is soon quite disoriented. The nun stops at a closed door and tells the man, "Please knock on this door." He does as he is told, and this door is answered by a nun holding a tin cup. This nun says, "Please place $50 into the cup, then go through the large wooden door at the end of this hallway." He gets $50 out of his wallet and places it into the cup.

He trots eagerly down the hall and slips through the door, pulling it shut behind him. As the door locks, he finds himself back in the parking lot facing another small sign:

GO IN PEACE, YOU HAVE JUST BEEN
SCREWED BY THE SISTERS OF MERCY

I Want A Second Opinion...

A man walking in the mountains stepped too close to the path's edge and started to fall. In desperation he grabbed a limb of a gnarly old tree. Full of fear he assessed his situation. He was about a hundred feet down a shear cliff and about nine hundred feet from the floor of the canyon below. If he should slip again, he'd plummet to his death. Full of fear he cried out, "Help me!" but there was no answer. Again and again he cried out, to no avail.

Finally he yelled, "Is anybody up there?"
A deep voice replied, "Yes, I'm up here."
"Who is it?"
"It's the Lord"
"Can you help me?"
"Yes, I can help. Let go."
Looking around, the man became full of panic. "What?!?!"
"Let go. I will catch you."
"Is anybody else up there?"

Salvation In A Small Tub...

It was time for Father John's Saturday night bath. The young nun, Sister Magdalene, had prepared the bathwater and towels just the way an old nun had instructed. Sister Magdalene was also instructed not to look at Fr. John's nakedness, to do whatever he told her, and to pray. The next morning the old nun asked about the bath.

"Oh, sister," said the young nun dreamily. "I've been saved."
"Saved? And how did that fine thing come about?" asked the old nun.
"When Fr. John was soaking in the tub, he asked me to wash him, and while I was washing him, he guided my hand down between his legs, where he said the Lord keeps the 'Key to Heaven.'"
"Did he now?" said the old nun evenly.
Sister Magdalene continued, "And Fr. John said if the 'Key to Heaven' fit my lock, the portals of Heaven would be opened to me and I would be assured of salvation and eternal peace. And then Father John guided his 'Key to Heaven' into my lock."

"Is that a fact?" said the old nun even more evenly.
"At first it hurt terribly, but Fr. John said the 'Pathway to Salvation' was often painful and that the glory of God would soon swell my heart with ecstasy. And it did. It felt so good being saved."

"That wicked old Devil!" said the old nun. "He told me it was Gabriel's horn, and I've been blowing it for 40 years!"

Ecumenical Plot...

The pope met with his cardinals to discuss a proposal from Benjamin Netanyahu, the former leader of Israel.

"Your Holiness," said one of the cardinals, "Mr. Netanyahu wants to challenge you to a game of golf to show the friendship and ecumenical spirit shared by the Jewish and Catholic faiths."

The pope thought it was a good idea, but he had never held a golf club in his hand. "Have we not," he asked, "a cardinal who can represent me against the former leader of Israel?"

"None who plays golf very well," a cardinal said. "But," he added, "there is Jack Nicklaus, an American golfer and a devout Catholic. We can make him a cardinal, then ask him to play Netanyahu as your personal representative. In addition to showing our spirit of cooperation, we'd also win the match."

Everyone agreed it was a good idea. The call was made. Nicklaus agreed to play. The day after the match he came to report the result.

"I've some good news and some bad news, Your Holiness," said the golfer. "Tell me the good news first, Cardinal Nicklaus," said the pope.

"Well, Your Holiness, I don't like to brag, but this was the best I had ever played. I must have been inspired from above. My drives were long and true and my putting was perfect. With all due respect my play was truly miraculous."

"There's bad news?" the pope asked. Nicklaus sighed. "I lost by three strokes to Rabbi Tiger Woods."

An Elder With The Right Idea...

A preacher was completing a temperance sermon. With great expression he said, "If I had all the beer in the world, I'd take it and throw it into the river." With even greater emphasis he said, "And if I had all the wine in the world, I'd take it and throw it into the river." And then finally, he said, "And if I had all the whiskey in the world, I'd take it and throw it into the river." He sat down.

The head elder then stood and announced, "For our closing song, let us sing Hymn 365, 'Shall We Gather at the River.'"

The Father, The Church, And The Holy Grocery...

Three couples—one elderly, one middle-aged, and one young newly-wed—were interviewing with the pastor, seeking admission to his church.

The pastor informed them that the only requirement was that they abstain from sex for two weeks and then report back to him.

The three couples returned to the pastor on the appointed day for their final interview. He asked the elderly couple, "Did you abstain from sex as required?" They replied that they had.

He next asked the middle-aged couple if they had followed the requirement for admission. They reported that they had, although during the second week it had been so difficult that one of them had had to sleep on the couch a couple of nights.

The pastor turned to the young couple and asked them if they had fulfilled the church's requirement of abstinence. "No" was the reply from the husband. "We did OK for several days, but it got more and more difficult. Then one day she was reaching for a can of soup on the top shelf and it fell to the floor. When she bent over to pick it up, I was overcome by lust, and I took her on the spot."

"Well," said the pastor, "you're not welcome in the church."

"I figured as much" the husband replied, "we're not welcome at Safeway anymore either."

A Confession That Leads...

Tommy goes into a confessional box and says, "Bless me, Father, for I have sinned. I have been with a loose woman." The priest says, "Is that you, Tommy?" "Yes, Father." "Who was the woman you were with?"

"I cannot tell you for I do not wish to sully her reputation."

The priest asks, "Was it Brenda O'Malley?" "No, Father." "Was it Fiona MacDonald?" "No, Father." "Was it Ann Brown?" "No, Father, I cannot tell you."

The priest says "I admire your perseverance, but you must atone for your sins. Your penance will be five 'Our Fathers' and four 'Hail Marys.'"

Tommy goes back to his pew. His buddy Sean slides over and asks "What happened?" Tommy replies, "I got five 'Our Fathers,' four 'Hail Marys,' and three good leads."

Church Bulletins In Need Of An Editor...

☦ Our next song is "Angels We Have Heard Get High."

☦ Don't let worry kill you—let the church help.

☦ Remember in prayer the many who are sick of our church and community.

☦ Weight Watchers will meet a 7 p.m. at the First Presbyterian Church. Please use large double door at the side entrance.

☦ The rosebud on the altar this morning is to announce the birth of David Alan Belzer, the sin of Rev. and Mrs. Julius Belzer.

☦ This afternoon there will be a meeting in the south and north ends of the church. Children will be baptized at both ends.

☦ Tuesday at 4 p.m. there will be an ice cream social. All ladies giving milk will please come early.

☦ This being Easter Sunday, we will ask Mrs. Lewis to come forward and lay an egg on the altar.

☦ Next Sunday we'll take a special collection for the new carpet. All those wishing to do something on the carpet should come forward and do so.

☦ The ladies of the church have castoff clothing of every kind. They can be seen in the church basement Saturday.

☦ Thursday night—Potluck Supper. Prayer and medication to follow.

☦ Eight new choir robes are currently needed, due to the addition of several new members and to the deterioration of some older ones.

☦ The senior choir invites any member of the congregation who enjoys sinning to join the choir.

☦ At the evening service tonight, the sermon topic will be "What is Hell?" Come early to listen to our choir practice.

☦ The Rev. Adams spoke briefly, much to the delight of his audience.

☦ The church is glad to have with us today guest minister the Rev. Stanley Green, who has Mrs. Green with him. After the service we request that all remain in the sanctuary for the Hanging of the Greens.

☦ The eighth graders will be presenting Shakespeare's *Hamlet* in the church basement on Friday at 7 p.m. The congregation is invited to attend this tragedy.

☦ The 1991 Spring Council Retreat will be hell May 10th and 11th.

☦ Pastor is on vacation. Massages can be given to church secretary.

☦ Please join us as we show our support for Amy and Alan in preparing for the girth of their first child.

☦ Scouts are saving aluminum cans, bottles, and other items to be recycled. Proceeds will be used to cripple children.

I'd Better Check That Out...

A minister told his congregation, "Next week I plan to preach about the sin of lying. To help you understand my sermon, I want you all to read Mark: 17."

The following Sunday as he prepared to deliver his sermon, the minister asked for a show of hands. He wanted to know how many had read Mark: 17. Every hand went up.

The minister smiled and said, "Mark has only 16 chapters. I shall now proceed with my sermon on the sin of lying."

Three Nuns And A Flasher...

Three nuns were riding in an elevator when it stopped at their floor. As the doors opened, a man flashed them.

The first nun, who was elderly, said, "Oh my, I think I'm going to have a stroke!"

The second nun, who was in her 50s, said, "Oh my, I think I am going to have a stroke also."

The third nun, who was only 22, said, "Well personally, I'm not going to touch it."

What Catholics Do At Church...

A man is struck by a bus on a busy street in New York City. He lies dying on the sidewalk as a crowd of spectators gathers. "A priest. Somebody get me a priest!" the man gasps. A policeman checks the crowd—no priest, no minister, no man of God of any kind.

"A PRIEST, PLEASE!" the dying man says again. Then out of the crowd steps a little old Jewish man who is at least 80 years old.

"Mr. Policeman," says the man, "I'm not a priest or even a Catholic. But for 50 years now I'm living behind St. Elizabeth's Catholic Church on First Avenue, and every night I'm listening to the Catholic litany. Maybe I can be of some comfort to this man."

The policeman agrees and leads the octogenarian to where the dying man lies. He kneels down, leans over the injured man, and says in a solemn voice:

"B-4. I-19. N-38. G-54. O-72."

The New Priest...

The new priest was so nervous at his first mass he could hardly speak. Before his second appearance in the pulpit, he asked the monsignor what he could do to relax. The monsignor said, "Next Sunday it may help if you put some vodka in the water pitcher. After a few sips, everything should go smoothly."

The following Sunday the new priest put the suggestion into practice and was able to talk up a storm. He felt great! However, upon returning to the rectory, he found this note from the monsignor:

Dear Father,

About your sermon, here are a few suggestions that may help:

1. *Next time sip rather than gulp.*
2. *There are 10 commandments, not 12.*
3. *There are 12 disciples, not 10.*
4. *We do not refer to the Cross as the "Big T."*
5. *The recommended grace before meals is not "Rub-a-dub-dub, thanks for the grub. Yeah, God!"*
6. *We do not refer to our Savior Jesus Christ and his Apostles as "J.C. and the Boys."*
7. *David slew Goliath. He did not "kick the shit out of him."*
8. *Moses parted the water in the Red Sea. He did not "pass water."*
9. *We don't refer to Judas as "El Finko."*
10. *The Pope is consecrated not castrated, and I don't believe we refer to him as "The Godfather."*
11. *When Jesus broke the bread at the Last Supper, he said, "Take this and eat it, for it is my body." He did not say "Eat me."*
12. *David was hit by a rock and knocked off his donkey. He wasn't "stoned off his ass."*
13. *The Father, Son, and the Holy Ghost are never referred to as "Big Daddy, Junior, and the Spook."*
14. *It is always the Virgin Mary, never "Mary with the Cherry."*
15. *Last, but not least, next Wednesday there will be a Taffy-Pulling contest at St. Peter's, not a "Peter-Pulling contest at St. Taffy's."*

I feel I'm diagonally parked in a parallel universe.

SCIENTISTS & ENGINEERS

Knowing Everything Can Be Dangerous...

A priest, a lawyer, and an engineer are about to be guillotined. The priest puts his head onto the block, they pull the rope, and nothing happens. He declares that he's been saved by divine intervention, and is released.

The lawyer is put onto the block, and again the rope doesn't release the blade. He claims he can't be executed twice for the same crime, and he is set free.

They grab the engineer and shove his head into the guillotine. He looks up at the release mechanism and says, "Wait a minute, I think I see your problem."

No One Said Engineers Were Normal...

Normal people believe if it ain't broke, don't fix it.
Engineers believe if it ain't broke, it doesn't have enough features.

No One Asks Theologians...

Engineers think that equations approximate the real world.
Scientists think that the real world approximates equations.
Mathematicians are unable to make the connection.

He Has One Spoke Missing...

While walking across campus, an engineering student encountered an E-school buddy riding on a shiny new motorcycle. "Where did you get such a rockin' bike?" asked the first student. The second replied, "I was walking along yesterday minding my own business when a beautiful woman rode up on this bike. She threw the bike to the ground, took off all her clothes, and said, "Take what you want." The second engineer nodded approvingly. "Good choice! The clothes probably wouldn't have fit."

Invitation Responses To The Scientists' Ball...

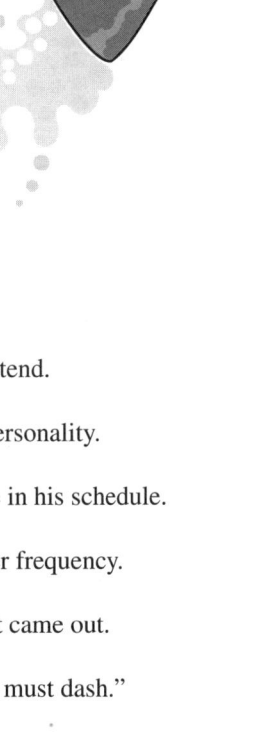

Ampere was worried he wasn't current.

Audubon said he'd have to wing it.

Boyle said he was under too much pressure.

Darwin waited to see what evolved.

Descartes said he'd think about it.

Dr. Jekyll declined. He hadn't been feeling himself lately.

Edison thought it would be illuminating.

Einstein thought it would be relatively easy to attend.

Gauss was asked to attend because of his magnetic personality.

Hawking tried to string enough time together to make space in his schedule.

Hertz said in the future he planned to attend with greater frequency.

Mendel said he'd put some things together to see what came out.

Morse replied, "I'll be there on the dot. Can't stop now, must dash."

Volta was electrified, and Archimedes was buoyant at the thought.

Wilbur Wright accepted, provided he and Orville could get a flight.

Watt reckoned it would be a good way to let off steam.

Newton planned to drop in.

Ohm resisted the idea.

Pierre and Marie Curie were radiating enthusiasm.

Pavlov was drooling at the thought.

Graduates...

The graduate with a science degree asks,
"Why does it work?"
The graduate with an engineering degree asks,
"How does it work?"
The graduate with an accounting degree asks,
"How much will it cost?"
The graduate with a political science degree asks,
"Do you want a side order of fries?"

The Freshman Viewpoint...

Three freshman engineering students were sitting around one day arguing about who might have designed the human body.

The first one said, "It must have been a mechanical engineer. The human body has all those levers and pivots and stuff—a mechanical engineer must have designed all that."

The second one said, "No, it had to have been an electrical engineer. The complex way the nerves are wired to the brain must have been designed by an electrical engineer."

Then the third one said, "No, it was a civil engineer. Who else would have run a waste water line through a recreational area?"

Scientific Study...

In 1991 the American government funded a scientific study to see why the head of a man's penis was larger than the shaft. After one year and $180,000, the study concluded that the reason the head was larger than the shaft was to give the man more pleasure during sex.

After the U.S. published the study, Germany decided to do its own study. After $250,000 and three years of research, the Germans concluded that the reason was to give the woman more pleasure during sex.

Poland, unsatisfied with those findings, conducted its own study. After three weeks and a cost of $75.47, the Polish scientists concluded that it was to keep a man's hand from flying off and hitting him in the forehead.

Way Too True...

A woman floating in a hot air balloon realizes she's lost. She reduces height and spots a man below. She lowers the balloon further and shouts, "Excuse me, can you help me? I promised my friend I would meet him half an hour ago, but I don't know where I am."

The man below says, "Yes. You are in a hot air balloon hovering approximately 30 feet above this field. You are between 40 and 42 degrees north latitude, and between 58 and 60 degrees west longitude."

"You must be an engineer," says the balloonist.

"I am," replies the man. "How did you know?"

"Well," says the balloonist, "everything you have told me is technically correct, but I have no idea what to make of your information, and the fact is I'm still lost."

The man below says, "You must be a manager."

"I am," replies the balloonist, "but how did you know?"

"Well," says the man, "you don't know where you are or where you're going. You've made a promise you have no idea how to keep, and you expect me to solve your problem. The fact is, you have the same problem you did before we met, but now somehow it's my fault."

What'dya Mean, Passion?

An architect, an artist, and an engineer were discussing whether it was better to spend time with the wife or a mistress. The architect said he enjoyed time with his wife, building a solid foundation for an enduring relationship.

The artist said he enjoyed time with his mistress, because of the passion and mystery he found there.

The engineer said, "I like both."

"Both?"

"Yeah. If you have a wife and a mistress, each will assume you are spending time with the other woman, and then you can go to the lab and get some work done!"

Just As I Suspected...

A bright young psychology student was assigned to help her professor conduct personality tests. The room was set up with various props to facilitate making assessments quickly.

The first person to enter the room began the test.
"How does this beaker of fluid look to you?"
First Person: "It's half empty."
The student assistant checked "pessimist."

Person two entered the room.
"How does this beaker of fluid look to you?"
Second Person: "It's half full."
The student assistant checked "optimist."

Person three entered the room.
"How does this beaker of fluid look to you?"
Third Person: "Looks as if you have twice as much glass as you need there."

The researcher looked totally blank. She went to consult with her professor. "Oh, him!" the professor said, "I forgot to warn you about engineers! They have no personalities."

One- And Two-Liners For Engineers...

What is the difference between mechanical engineers and civil engineers?
Mechanical engineers build weapons. Civil engineers build targets.

The two most common elements in the universe are hydrogen and stupidity.

Ever wonder what the speed of lightning would be if it didn't zigzag.

Quantum mechanics—the dreams stuff is made of.

Two hydrogens walk into a bar. The first one says, "Oh, no. I lost an electron!" The second one says, "Are you sure?" The first one says, "Yeah, I'm positive."

The only jogging I do now is to my memory.

Senior Citizens Jokes

You Know You're Not A Kid Anymore When . . .

You're asleep, but others worry that you're dead.
You can live without sex but not without glasses.
Your back goes out more than you do.
You quit trying to hold in your stomach,
no matter who walks into the room.
You buy a compass for the dash of your car.
You're proud of your lawn mower.
Your best friend is dating someone half his age
and isn't breaking any laws.
You call Olan Mills before they call you.
Your arms are too short to read the newspaper.
You sing along with the elevator music.
You would rather go to work than stay home sick.
You constantly talk about the price of gasoline.
You enjoy hearing about other people's operations.
You make an appointment to see the dentist.
You no longer think of speed limits as a challenge.
Neighbors borrow your tools.
People who call at 9 p.m. ask, "Did I wake you?"
You dream about prunes.
You answer a question with "Because I said so!"
You send money to PBS.
You still buy 33 rpm records, and you think a CD is a certificate of deposit.
The end of your tie doesn't come anywhere near the top of your pants.
You take a metal detector to the beach.
You wear black socks with sandals.
You know what the word "equity" means.
You can't remember the last time you lay on the floor to watch TV.
Your ears are hairier than your head.
You talk about "good grass," and you're referring to someone's lawn.
You get into a heated argument about pension plans.
You subscribe to cable for the weather channel.
You can go bowling without drinking.
You have a party, and the neighbors don't even know it.

Miss Bea...

Miss Bea, in her 80s, was much admired for her sweetness and kindness to all. One early spring afternoon her pastor came to call. She welcomed him into her Victorian parlor.

She invited the pastor to have a seat while she prepared tea. As he sat in the parlor, the young minister noticed a cut glass bowl filled with water sitting atop the old pump organ. Imagine his shock and surprise when he saw floating in the water—of all things—a condom! He could not imagine what Miss Bea must be thinking—or doing! But he didn't know how to ask about the strange sight.

When she returned with tea and cookies, the two began chatting. The pastor tried to stifle his curiosity about the bowl and its strange floater, but soon it got the best of him. He could resist no longer. "Miss Bea" he said, "I wonder if you could tell me about your bowl?"

"Oh yes" she replied, "isn't it wonderful? I was walking downtown last fall, and I found this little package. It said to put it on your organ, keep it wet, and it would prevent disease. And, you know, I think it's working! I haven't had a cold all winter."

Expecting...

After marrying a much younger woman, a 93-year-old man visited his doctor and announced his wife was expecting a baby. "Let me tell you a story," said the doctor. An absentminded fellow went hunting, but instead of a gun, he picked up an umbrella. Suddenly a tiger charged toward him. Pointing his umbrella at the tiger, he shot and killed the animal on the spot."

"Impossible!" exclaimed the old man. "Somebody must have shot from the side!"

"Exactly," replied the doctor.

The Old Man And The Moped...

A hip young rich man heads out to buy a new Ferrari GTO. It is the best, most expensive car in the world, costing about $500,000. While he is taking it out for a spin, he stops at a red light. An old man on a moped (both of which look to be about 90) pulls up next to him. The old man looks over the sleek shiny surface of the car and asks, "What kind of car you got there, sonny?"

The young man replies, "A new Ferrari GTO. It costs about a half million dollars!"
"That's a lot of money," says the shocked old man. "Why does it cost so much?"
"Because this car can go up to 320 miles an hour!" states the cool dude proudly.
The moped driver asks, "May I take a look inside?"
"Sure," replies the owner.
So the old man pokes his head in the window and looks around. Leaning back on his moped, he says, "That's a pretty nice car, all right!"

Just as the light changes, the guy decides to show the old man what his car can do. He floors it, and within 30 seconds the speedometer reads nearly 200 mph. Suddenly, he notices a dot in his rear view mirror. It seems to be getting closer! He slows down to see what it could be and suddenly, whhhoooosshhh! Something whips by him, going much faster! "What on earth could be going faster than my Ferrari?" the young man asks himself.

Then, ahead of him he sees a dot coming toward him. Whoooooosh! It goes by again, heading the opposite direction! And it looks a lot like the old man on the moped!

"Couldn't be," thinks the guy. "How could a moped outrun a Ferrari?"

Again, he sees a dot in his rear view mirror! Whooooosh Ka-BbblaMMM! It plows into the back of his car, demolishing the rear end. The young man jumps out, and it IS the old man!!! Of course the moped and the old man are hurt. The driver runs up to the injured old man and says, "You're hurt! Is there anything I can do for you?"

The old man moans and replies, "Yes, unhook my suspenders from your side mirror!"

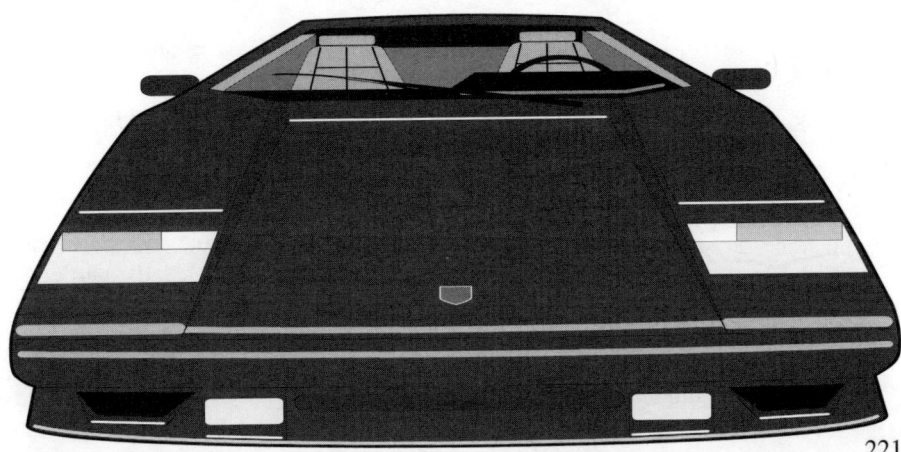

Priorities Change With Time...

A policeman noticed an old lady standing on a street corner during a sudden windstorm. She was bracing herself by holding a lightpost with one hand, and with her other hand she was holding her hat snugly against her head. Unfortunately, a strong gust blew her dress upward, and it continued to flap in the wind, exposing her privates for everyone to see.

The policeman said, "Lady, everybody is looking at what you've got. Don't you think that pulling your dress down is more important than worrying about your hat?"

"Look, sonny. What these people are looking at is 85 years old! But my hat is BRAND NEW!"

Whoosh...

Two elderly gentlemen who had been without sex for several years decided they wanted to visit a cathouse for some tail. When they arrived, the madam took one look at them and decided she wasn't going to waste any of her girls on these two decrepid old men.

Instead she put a "blow-up" doll in each man's room and left them to their business. After the two men were finished and had started home, they got to talking. The first man said, "I think the girl I had was dead. She never moved or said a word or even groaned. How was yours?"

The second man replied, "I think mine was a witch." The first man asked, "Why's that?" "Well," said the second man, "when I nibbled on her breast, she let out a long fart, and flew out the window!"

Call 'Em The Way You See 'Em...

The wealthy old gentleman and his wife were celebrating their 35th wedding anniversary. Their three grown sons had joined them for dinner. The old man was irritated when he discovered none of the boys had bothered to bring a gift. After the meal he drew them aside.

"You're all grown men," he said, "and old enough to hear this. Your mother and I have never been legally married."

"What?" gasped one of the sons. "Do you mean to say we're all bastards?"

"Yes," snapped the old man, "and cheap ones, too!"

We've Been Wondering Who That Was...

An 80-year-old man went for his annual checkup, and the doctor said, "Friend, for your age you're in the best shape I've seen."

The old feller replied, "Yep. It comes from clean living."

The doctor asked, "What makes you say that?"

The old man replied, "If I didn't live a good clean life, the Lord wouldn't turn the bathroom light on for me every time I get up in the middle of the night."

The doc was concerned. "You mean when you get up at night to go to the bathroom, the Lord Himself turns on the light for you?"

"Yep," the old man said, "Whenever I get up to go to the bathroom, the Lord turns on the light for me."

The doctor didn't say anything else, but when the old man's wife came in for her checkup, he felt he had to let her know what her husband had said. "I just want you to know your husband is in fine physical shape, but I'm worried about his mental condition. He told me that every night when he gets up to go to the bathroom, the Lord turns on the light for him."

"He what?" she cried.

"He said every night when he gets up to go to the bathroom, the Lord turns on the light for him."

"Aha!!!" she exclaimed. "So he's the one who's been peeing in the refrigerator!"

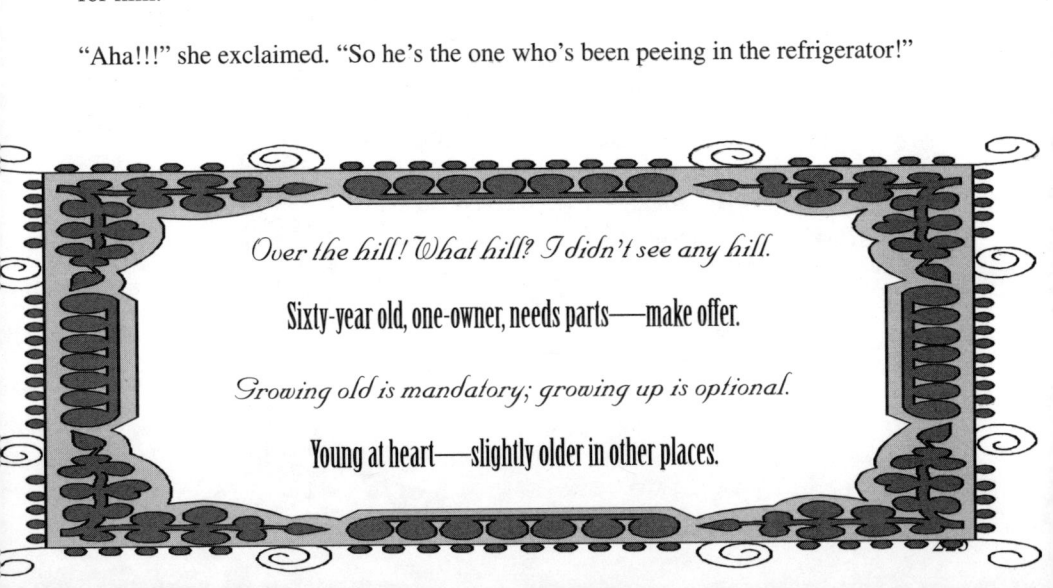

Over the hill! What hill? I didn't see any hill.

Sixty-year old, one-owner, needs parts—make offer.

Growing old is mandatory; growing up is optional.

Young at heart—slightly older in other places.

Dad???

A young punker gets onto the crosstown bus. He has spiked multicolored hair green, purple, and orange. His clothes are a tattered mix of leather rags. His legs are bare, and he's without shoes. His entire face and body are riddled with pierced jewelry, and his earrings are big bright feathers.

He sits down in the only vacant seat. An old man directly across from the kid glares at him for the next 10 miles. Finally, the punk gets self-conscious and barks at the old man, "What are you looking at, you old fart. Didn't you ever do anything wild when you were young?"

Without missing a beat, the old man replies, "Yes. Back when I was young and in the navy, I got really drunk one night in Singapore and had sex with a parrot. I thought maybe you were my son."

The more you complain, the longer God lets you live.

Wrinkled was not one of the things I wanted to be when I grew up.

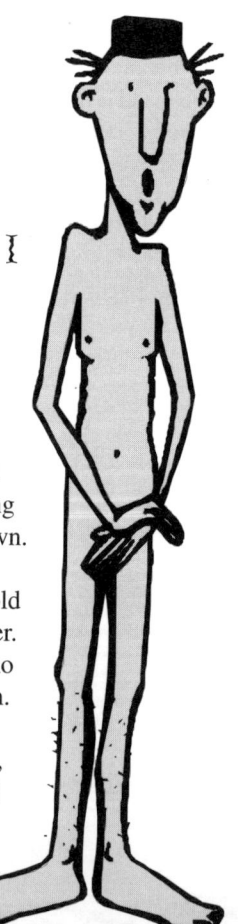

Stiff Neck...

A man was walking down the street when he noticed his grandpa sitting on his front porch in a rocking chair, wearing nothing from the waist down.

"Grandpa, what are you doing?" he exclaimed. The old man looked off into the distance and did not answer. "Grandpa, what are you doing sitting out here with no pants on?" he asked again.

The old man looked slyly at him and said, "This was your Grandma's idea! Last week I sat out here with no shirt, and my neck got stiff."

Memory's The First Thing To Go...

An 85-year-old man marries a lovely 25-year-old woman. Because her new husband is so old, the woman decides on their wedding night they should have separate suites. She is concerned that the old fellow might overexert.

After the festivities she prepares herself for bed and for the knock on the door she is expecting. Sure enough the knock comes, and there is her groom ready for action.

They unite in conjugal bliss. He takes his leave, and she prepares to go to sleep for the night. A few minutes later there's a knock on the door, and there the old guy is again, ready for more action. Somewhat surprised, she consents to further coupling, which is again successful, after which the octogenarian bids her a fond good night and leaves once more.

She is certainly ready for slumber at this point and is close to sleep for the second time when there is another knock at the door. There he is again, fresh as a 25-year-old and ready for more. Once again they do the horizontal boogie.

As they're lying in the afterglow, the young bride says to him, "I am really impressed that a guy your age has enough juice to go for it three times. I've been with men less than half your age who were only good for one."

The old guy looks puzzled and turns to her and says, "Was I already here?"

Hairspray...

A little boy and his grandfather are raking leaves in the yard. The little boy finds an earthworm trying to get back into its hole. He says, "Grandpa, I bet I can put that worm back in that hole."

The grandfather replies, "I'll bet you $5 you can't. It's too wiggly and limp to put back into that little hole." The little boy runs into the house and returns with a can of hairspray. After he sprays the worm until it's straight and stiff as a board, he easily slips it back into the hole. The grandfather hands the little boy $5, grabs the hairspray, and runs into the house. Thirty minutes later the grandfather comes back out and hands the little boy another $5.

The little boy says, "Grandpa, you already gave me $5." The grandfather replies, "I know. That was from me. This one is from your grandma."

If love is blind... why is lingerie so popular?
— Steven Wright

Sex Jokes

Camelot...

King Arthur was worried about leaving Queen Guinevere alone with all the horny knights of the Round Table. So he went to Merlin for advice. After Arthur explained his predicament, the wizard looked thoughtful. He said that he'd see if he could come up with a solution and asked the king to return in a week.

A week later, back in Merlin's laboratory, the good wizard showed Arthur his latest invention. It was a chastity belt, except it had a large hole in the most obvious place.

"This won't work, Merlin!" the king exclaimed, "Look at this opening. How can this protect the Queen?"

"Ah, sire, observe," said Merlin, as he searched his cluttered work bench. He located his most worn-out wand and inserted it in the gaping aperture of the chastity belt. SWISH, CHOP! The small guillotine blade instantly sliced the wand neatly in two.

"Merlin, you're a genius!" said the grateful monarch, "Now I can leave, knowing that my Queen is fully protected."

After putting Guinevere into the device, King Arthur set out upon his quest. Several years passed before he returned to Camelot. Immediately he assembled all his knights in the courtyard and had them drop their trousers for an informal "short arms" inspection. His worst fears were realized. All but one of the penises had been either amputated or damaged. Except for Sir Galahad.

"Sir Galahad," exclaimed King Arthur, "You are the one and only true knight! Only you amongst all the nobles has been true to me. What is it in my power to grant you? Name it and it is yours!"

But Sir Galahad was speechless.

Soldier? Soldier? What Soldier?

Mr. Johnson got himself a new secretary. She was young, sweet, and very polite. One day while taking dictation, she noticed Mr. Johnson's fly was open. As she left the room, she said, "Mr. Johnson, your barracks door is open." At first, he did not understand the remark, but later he happened to look down. He saw his zipper was open. He decided to have some fun with his secretary. Calling her back in, he asked, "By the way, Miss Jones, when you said my barracks door was open this morning, did you also notice a soldier standing at attention?" The secretary, who was quite witty replied, "Why, no sir, all I saw was a little disabled veteran sitting on two duffel bags."

One Hump Or Two...

There's a new commander at a French foreign legion base and the captain is showing him around all the buildings. After making the rounds, the commander says to the captain, "Wait a minute. You haven't shown me that small blue building over there. What's that used for?" The captain says, "Well sir, you see that there are no women around. Whenever the men feel the need of a woman, they go there and use the camel." "Enough!" says the commander in disgust.

Two weeks later the commander himself starts to feel the need for a woman. He goes to the captain and says, "Tell me something, Captain." Lowering his voice and glancing furtively around, he asks, "Is the camel free soon?" The captain says, "Let me see." He opens his book. "Yes, sir, the camel is free tomorrow afternoon at two o'clock." The commander says, "Put me down for two then." The next day at two o'clock the commander goes to the little blue building and opens the door.

Inside he finds the cutest camel he's ever seen. Next to the camel is a little stool. So he closes the door behind him and puts the stool directly behind the camel. He stands on the stool, drops his pants, and begins to have sex with the camel. A minute later the captain walks in. "Ahem, begging your pardon sir," says the captain, "but wouldn't it be wiser to ride the camel into town and find a woman like all the other men?"

Be Loud And Clear...

Two friends are playing golf when one pulls out a cigar. He doesn't have a lighter, so he asks his friend for one.

"Here you go," he replies, as he reaches into his golf bag and pulls out a 12-inch BIC lighter.

"Wow !" says his friend, "where did you get that monster?"

"From my genie."

"You have a genie?" he asks.

"Yes, he's right here in my golf bag.
He opens his golf bag, and out pops the genie.

The friend says, "I'm a good friend of your master. Will you grant me one wish?"

"Yes, I will," the genie says.

So he asks the genie for a million bucks, and the genie hops back into the golf bag and leaves him standing there waiting for his million bucks.

Suddenly the sky begins to darken, and they hear the sound of a million ducks flying overhead.

The friend tells his golfing partner, "I asked for a million *bucks*, not *ducks*!"

He answers, "I forgot to tell you the genie is hard of hearing. Do you really think I asked him for a 12-inch BIC?"

The Shower...

A beautiful young woman gets out of the shower, wraps a towel around herself, and tells her husband to come into the shower. As he enters, the doorbell rings. The wife says she'll go downstairs.

When she opens the door, she sees her neighbor, Bill, whose mouth opens wide at the sight of her wrapped in a towel. He pulls out two $100 bills and tells her they're hers if she will just let the towel fall to her waist. She thinks, "why not." With that she drops the towel and takes the money.

Bill gasps at the sight and shows her two more hundreds. He offers them if she'll let the towel go altogether. She thinks she has come this far so, what the heck. She drops the towel. Bill looks up and down for a minute, thanks her, and leaves.

When she gets back upstairs, her husband asks who was at the door. She says, "Just Bill."

The husband replies, "Did he say anything about the $400 he owes me?"

Looking For Natalie...

The madam opened the brothel door to see an elderly Jewish man. His clothes were dishevelled and he looked "needy."

"May I help you?" asked the madam. "I want Natalie," the old man replied. "Sir, Natalie is one of our most expensive ladies. Perhaps you'd like someone else?" "No, I want Natalie." Just then, Natalie appeared and announced to the old man that she charged $1,000 an hour. The man never blinked, reached into his pocket, and handed her 10 $100 bills. The two went up to a room for a delightful hour.

The next night he appeared again and demanded Natalie. Natalie explained that no one had ever come back two nights in a row, there were no discounts, the fee was still $1,000 an hour. Again the old man took out the money. The two went up to her room, and he calmly left an hour later. When he showed up the third consecutive night, no one could believe it. Again he handed Natalie the money and up to the room they went. At the end of the hour Natalie questioned the old man. "No one has ever used my services three nights in a row. Where are you from?"

The old man replied, "I am from Minsk."

"Really," replied Natalie. "I have a sister who lives there."

"I know," said the old man. "She gave me $3,000 to give to you."

Sheer Lingerie...

A man goes to Frederick's of Hollywood. He wants to buy his wife the sheerest lingerie he can find. The woman behind the counter shows him a revealing outfit.

"This is $200," she says.

"I want one that's sheerer," he says.

"This one is $350."

"I want one even sheerer than that."

"This one is the sheerest that we have. It's $500."

"I'll take it!"

The man goes home to his wife and shows it to her, saying, "Go put this on, and come down to model it for me."

His wife goes upstairs, opens the box, and thinks, "This thing is so see-through that the old coot won't even notice if I'm wearing it or not. I can take this back for a refund, and he won't know the difference."

So his wife comes out wearing nothing at all and strikes a pose at the top of the stairs. "So, how do you like it?" she says.

"Damn, you'd think for $500 they'd iron the damn thing."

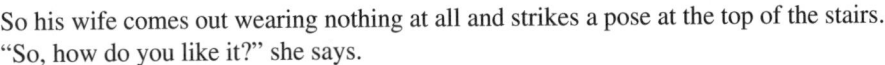

Ever Try Whining And Crying?

Two buddies were sharing drinks while discussing their wives.
"Do you and your wife ever do it doggie style?" asked one.
"Well, not exactly," his friend replied.
"She's more into the trick dog aspect of it."
"Oh, I see. Kinky, huh?"
"Well, not exactly."
"I sit up and beg, and she rolls over and plays dead."

Magic Sandals...

A married couple on holiday in Pakistan passed a small sandal shop. A gentleman within said, "Greetings! Come in, come into my humble shop." So the couple walked inside. The Pakistani owner said, "I have special sandals I think you'll like. They will make you as wild at sex as a great desert camel."

After hearing this, the woman was very interested in buying the sandals, but her husband felt he really didn't need them, believing he was already a sex god.

The husband said to the man, "How can sandals make you wild at sex?" The Pakistani man replied, "Just try them on."

So the husband, after much badgering from his wife, finally conceded to try them. He put the sandals on and got a wild look in his eyes, something his wife had not seen in many years—raw sexual power. Instantly the husband rushed the Pakistani man, threw him onto a table, and started tearing at the guy's pants.

While being attacked, the shopkeeper kept screaming, "Stop! Stop! You've got them on the wrong feet!"

The Penis Tax...

The only thing that the I.R.S. has not taxed is the penis. This is due to the fact that 40% of the time it's hanging around unemployed, 20% of the time it's pissed off, 30% of the time it's hard-up, 10% of the time it's in the hole. On top of all this, it has two dependents, and they're both nuts.

Therefore, starting January 1, 2000, penises will be taxed according to size ! ! ! To determine the right category for you, please consult the chart below.

Penis Tax Bill

10 to 12 inches................Luxury Tax............ $50.00
8 to 10 inches.................Pole Tax................. $30.00
6 to 8 inches...................Privilege Tax..........$15.00
4 to 6 inches...................Nuisance Tax......... $ 5.00

PLEASE NOTE : Anyone under four inches is eligible for a refund.
PLEASE DO NOT ASK FOR AN EXTENSION ! ! ! ! ! ! !

Males exceeding 12 inches must file Capital Gains

P.S. Dammit!! I've got to file Capital Gains.

The height of conceit is having an orgasm and calling out your own name.

Sex is not the answer.
Sex is the question.
"Yes," is the answer.

Sex is the most fun you can have without laughing.

A Bird In The Hand...

One day Pinnochio and his girlfriend were in bed doing what girls and wooden boys do. Later, as they were cuddling, Pinnochio could tell that something was bothering his girlfriend. So he asked, "What's the matter, baby?"

Pinnochio's girlfriend gave a big sigh and replied, "You're probably the best guy I've ever met, but every time we make love, you give me splinters."

Her remark bothered Pinnochio greatly, so the next day he went to seek advice from his creator, Gepetto. Gepetto could tell something was troubling Pinnochio, so he asked if he could help. As Pinnochio revealed his dilemma, Gepetto searched for a solution. Eventually he suggested that sandpaper might be able to "smooth out" Pinnochio's relationship with his girlfriend. Pinnochio happily accepted Gepetto's innovative solution and went on his way.

Gepetto did not hear from the boy for quite a while, so he assumed the sandpaper had solved Pinnochio's problem.

A couple of weeks later Gepetto was in town having blades sharpened when he saw Pinnochio buying all the shop's sandpaper. Gepetto remarked, "So, Pinnochio, things must be going well with you and the girls."

To which Pinnochio replied,

"GIRLS? WHO NEEDS GIRLS???"

Salt...

A man and a woman are sitting next to each other in the first class section of an airline. The man sneezes, pulls out his penis, and wipes the tip. The woman can't believe what she just saw. She decides she must have been hallucinating. A few minutes pass. The man sneezes again. Immediately, he pulls out his penis and wipes the tip. The woman is beside herself. She stares in disbelief. After a few more minutes, the man sneezes for the third time. He takes out his penis and wipes the tip again. The woman, who has had enough, turns to the man and says, "Three times you've sneezed, and each time you've removed your penis from your pants and wiped the tip! What kind of degenerate are you?"

The man replies, "I'm sorry I disturbed you, ma'am. I have a very rare medical condition. Whenever I sneeze, I have an orgasm."

The woman sheepishly says, "Really! What are you taking for it?"

The man looks over at her and says, "Pepper!"

Solidarity Forever...

A dedicated union worker recently attended a labor convention in Sydney. As you might expect, he decided to check out the nearby brothels.

When he got to the first one, he asked the madam, "Is this a unionized house?"
"No." she replied, "It isn't."

"Well, if I pay you $100, what cut does the girl get?"
"The house gets $80, and the girl get $20."

Mightily offended at such blatantly unfair dealings, the man stomped down the street in search of a more equitable, if not unionized, shop. Finally he reached a brothel where the madam responded, "Why, yes sir, this is a union house."

"At last!" he said. "If I pay you $100, what cut does the girl get?"

"The house gets $20 and the girl get $80."

"That's more like it," the union man said, and he promptly handed over his $100. He looked around the room and pointed to a stunningly attractive blonde. "I'd like her for the night."

"I'm sure you would, sir," said the madam smoothly. Then, gesturing to an obese 65-year-old woman in the corner, "but Ethel has seniority!"

The Mailman's Treat...

It was George the mailman's last day on the job after 35 years of carrying the mail through all kinds of weather to the same neighborhood. When he arrived at the first house on his route, he was greeted by the whole family, who roundly and soundly congratulated him and sent him on his way with a tidy gift envelope.

At the second house, the husband presented him with a box of fine cigars. The folks at the third house handed him a selection of terrific fishing lures.

At the fourth house he was met at the door by a strikingly beautiful woman in a revealing negligee. She took him by the hand, gently led him through the door and up the stairs to the bedroom. There she blew his mind with the most passionate love he had ever experienced! When he had enough, they went downstairs. She fixed him a giant breakfast of eggs, potatoes, ham, sausage, blueberry waffles, and freshly squeezed orange juice. When he was truly satisfied, she made a fresh pot of steaming coffee. As she was pouring, he noticed a dollar bill sticking out from under the cup's bottom edge.

"All of this was just too wonderful for words," he said, "but what's the dollar for?"

"Well," she said, "last night, I told my husband that today would be your last day and that we should do something special for you. I asked him what to give you, and he said; "Screw him. Give him a dollar."
"The breakfast was my idea!!"

It's The Other Rodeo Ride...

Two cowboys are sitting in a bar when one asks the other,

"Hey, have you heard of the new sex position called *Rodeo*?"

The other says, "No, what is it?"
"You mount your wife from behind, reach around and cup her breasts, and say, 'Gee, these are almost as nice as your sister's. Then see if you can stay on for eight seconds."

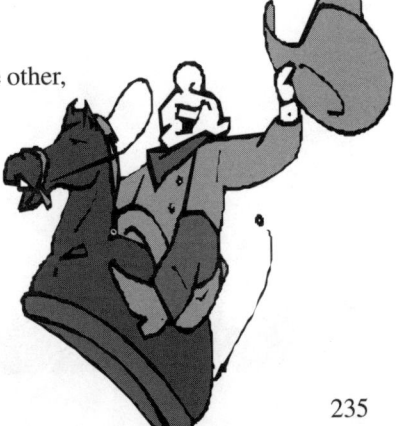

So, These Three Dogs Were Talking...

Three Labrador retrievers—a brown, a yellow, and a black—are sitting in the waiting room at the vet's office when they strike up a conversation.

The black Lab turns to the brown and says, "So why are you here?"

The brown Lab replies, "I'm a pisser. I piss on everything—the sofa, the drapes, the cat, the kids. But the final straw was last night when I pissed in the middle of my owner's bed."

The black Lab says, "So what is the vet going to do?"

"Gonna give me Prozac," comes the reply from the brown Lab. "All the vets are prescribing it. It works for everything."

The black Lab then turns to the yellow Lab and asks, "Why are you here?"

The yellow Lab says, "I'm a digger. I dig under fences, I dig up flowers and trees, I dig just for the hell of it. When I'm inside, I dig up the carpets. But I went over the line last night when I dug a great big hole in my owner's couch."

"So what are they going to do to you?" the black Lab inquires.

"Looks like Prozac for me too," the dejected yellow Lab says. The yellow Lab then turns to the black Lab and asks why he's at the vet's office.

"I'm a humper," the black Lab says. "I'll hump anything. I'll hump the cat, a pillow, the table, fire hydrants, whatever. I want to hump everything I see. Yesterday, my owner had just gotten out of the shower and was bending down to dry her toes, and I just couldn't help myself. I hopped onto her back and started humping away."

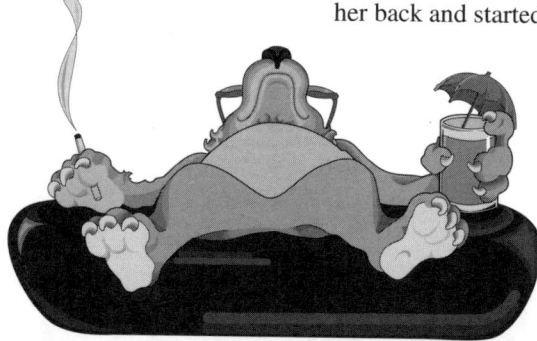

The yellow and brown Labs exchange a sad glance and say, "So, it looks like Prozac for you too, huh?"

The black Lab says, "Hell, No!! I'm here to get my nails clipped."

The Other White Meat...

A priest and a rabbi found themselves sharing a compartment on a train. After a while the priest put down his book and opened a conversation by asking, "I know in your religion you're not supposed to eat pork. But have you really never even tasted it?" The rabbi closed his newspaper and responded, "I must tell you the truth. Yes, I have, on the odd occasion."

The rabbi took a turn at interrogation and asked, "I know that in your religion, you're supposed to be celibate, but..."

The priest interjected, "Yes, I know what you're going to ask. And yes, I have succumbed to temptation once or twice."

The two resumed their reading. There was silence for a while.

Then the rabbi peeked around his newspaper and said, "Better than pork, isn't it?!"

Pickles...

Bill worked in a pickle factory. He had been employed there for a number of years when he came home one day to confess to his wife that he had a terrible compulsion. He had an urge to stick his penis into the pickle slicer. His wife suggested that he see a sex therapist, but Bill indicated that he'd be too embarrassed. He vowed to overcome the compulsion on his own. One day a few weeks later, Bill came home absolutely ashen. His wife could see at once that something was seriously wrong. "What's the matter, Bill?" she asked.

"Do you remember that I told you how I had this tremendous urge to put my penis into the pickle slicer?"

"Oh, Bill, you didn't."
"Yes, I did."
"My God, Bill, what happened?"

"They fired me."

"No, Bill. I mean, what happened with the pickle slicer?"

"Oh. They fired her too."

Golfers play with dimpled balls.

Sports Jokes

Wanna See My Lie?

A couple met on holiday at Hilton Head and fell in love. They were discussing how they would continue the relationship after their vacations. "It's only fair to warn you, Jody," Bill said. "I'm a golf nut. I live, eat, sleep, and breathe golf."

Jody said, "Well, since you're being honest, so will I." "I'm a hooker."

"I see." he said. Then, brightening, he smiled. "It's probably because you're not keeping your wrists straight when you hit the ball."

You Can Fool Some Of Them All Of The Time...

A man tells his wife he's going out to buy cigarettes. When he gets to the store, he finds it closed. So he ends up going down to the local bar to use the vending machine. While there, he drinks a few beers and begins talking to this beautiful girl. He buys her a few beers, and the next thing he knows he's in the girl's apartment having a good time. The next thing he knows it's 3 a.m.

Oh, my God, my wife's going to kill me!" he exclaims. "Quick, give me some talcum powder!" She gives him a tin, and he rubs powder all over his hands. When he gets home, his wife has been waiting, and she's furious.

"Where the hell have you been?"

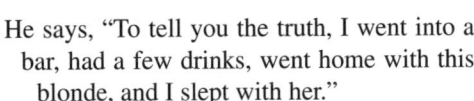

He says, "To tell you the truth, I went into a bar, had a few drinks, went home with this blonde, and I slept with her."

Let me see your hands!" she demands. He shows his wife his powdery hands.

"Damn liar. You were out bowling again!"

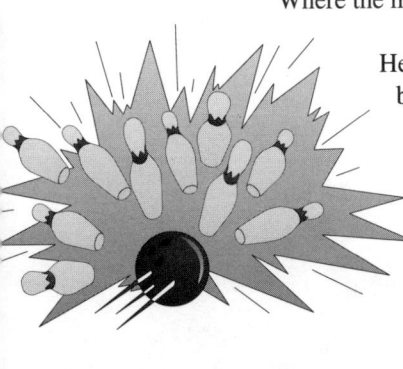

The Golfer And The Cow...

A foursome is playing the last hole when the final golfer drives off the tee only to hook into a cow pasture. He advises his friends to play on without him, and they all agree to meet at the clubhouse.

He finally limps in, dishevelled, bloody, and badly beaten up. His friends all want to know what happened to him.

He explains that he walked over to the cow pasture but could not find his ball. He noticed a cow wringing her tail in obvious pain. He approached, lifted her tail, and saw a golf ball solidly embedded. It was a yellow ball, so he knew it wasn't his.

At that point a woman came from the bushes, apparently searching for her lost golf ball. The helpful male golfer lifted the cow's tail and asked, "Does this look like yours?"

That was the last thing he could remember.

Q: What has four legs and one ear?
A: Mike Tyson's dog.

Want That With Fries?

"Hey, I just heard you can download the entire Tyson-Holyfield fight from the Internet," one boxing fan mentioned to another.

"Really?" said the other man. "How much memory does it take?"

"Very little," replied the first man. "Just two bytes."

Don't Chew!

Billy Bob and Jethro decide to go ice fishing. On arriving at the lake early one morning, they cut two holes in the ice and drop their lines into the water. After fishing for a few hours, Billy Bob has caught dozens of fish, but Jethro hasn't even gotten a bite. Jethro asks, "Billy Bob, what's your secret?"

Billy Bob answers, "Mmu motta meep da mmrms mmrm."

Jethro asks, "What did you say?"

Billy Bob responds, "Mmu motta meep da mmrms mmrm."

Jethro again asks, "What?"

Billy Bob spits into his hand and says, "You gotta keep the worms warm!"

Q: Why does Mike Tyson cry during sex?
A: Mace will do that to you.

Everyone Needs Priorities...

Two men were golfing one summer day. As one was about to step onto the 18th green and attempt a putt, he noticed an approaching funeral procession. The golfer stepped back from his putt, removed his hat, and bowed his head to show respect for the deceased. After the procession passed, he replaced his cap and sank his putt. His partner was impressed by this show of respect and noted to mention it.

Afterwards, as the golfers relaxed in the clubhouse with a drink and totaled their scores, the second golfer mentioned the event on the 18th hole. "You know, Fred, that was a very decent thing you did, showing respect like that. I was touched."

Fred simply shrugged his shoulders and replied, "Well, it was the least I could do. After all I was married to her for 40 years."

C'mon Charlie...

Robert goes golfing every Saturday. One Saturday he comes home three hours late. His wife asks him, "What took you so long?"

The guy says, "That's the worst game of golf I ever played. We got up to the first tee. Charlie hit a hole-in-one and immediately dropped dead of a heart attack."

The guy's wife says, "That's terrible!"

The guy agrees. "I know. For the rest of the game, it was hit the ball, drag Charlie, hit the ball, drag Charlie, hit the ball, drag..."

How Divers Avoid Shark Attacks...

1. Never leave Kansas.
2. Roll in manure before diving. Sharks hate anything breaded.
3. Always dive with a buddy. When sharks approach, point to buddy.
4. Dive with a briefcase. Sharks may mistake you for an attorney and leave you alone out of professional courtesy.

Double-Digit IQ Required To Play...

A football coach looked over to his star player and said, "I know I'm not supposed to let you play since you failed math, but we need you in there. How about I ask you a math question to prove you know your math? Then you can play."

The player agreed, and the coach asked the following question. "OK, what's 2+2?"

The player thought for a moment and then answered, "4." Suddenly, all the other players on the team began screaming, "Come on coach, give him another chance!"

Some Buddy!

Q: Why do buddy divers always carry a knife?
A: If confronted by a mean looking shark, you can always stab your buddy and swim away.

The Celestial Golf Game...

Moses, Jesus, and an old man are golfing. Moses steps up to the tee and hits the ball. It goes sailing over the fairway and lands in the water trap. Moses parts the water and chips the ball onto the green.

Jesus steps up to the tee and hits the ball. It goes sailing over the fairway and lands in the water trap. Jesus walks on the water and chips the ball onto the green.

The old man steps up to the tee and hits the ball. It goes sailing over the fairway and heads for the water trap. But, just before it falls into the water, a fish jumps up and grabs the ball in its mouth. As the fish is falling back down into the water, an eagle swoops down and grabs the fish in its claws. The eagle flies over the green, where a lightning bolt shoots from the sky and barely misses it. Startled, the eagle drops the fish. When the fish hits the ground, the ball pops out of its mouth and rolls into the hole for a hole-in-one.

Jesus then turns to the old man and says, "Dad, if you don't stop fooling around and play fair, we won't bring you next time."

Never On Sunday...

"I didn't see you in church last Sunday, Nigel. I hear you were out playing football instead"

"That's not true, Vicar. And I've got the fish to prove it!"

Never Assume Competence...

It's a sunny Saturday morning on the golf course, and a golfer is beginning his pre-shot routine. While visualizing his upcoming shot, a voice from the clubhouse loudspeaker says, "Will the gentleman on the ladies' tee please back up to the men's tee?"

He's still deep into his routine and seemingly impervious to the interruption.

Again the announcer, "Will the MAN on the WOMEN'S tee kindly back up to the men's tee?"

He has had enough. He shouts, "Will the announcer in the clubhouse kindly shut the hell up and let me play my second shot!"

VENI, VEDI, VISA!
I CAME.
I SAW.
I did a little shopping!

Women

Tastes Just Like Chicken...

Once upon a time in a land far away a beautiful, independent, self-assured princess happened upon a frog as she sat contemplating ecological issues on the shores of an unpolluted pond in a verdant meadow near her castle.

The frog hopped into the princess's lap and said, "Elegant Lady, I was once a handsome prince until an evil witch cast a spell upon me. One kiss from you and I shall turn back into the dapper young prince I am. Then, my sweet, we can marry and set up housekeeping in yon castle with my mother, where you can prepare my meals, clean my clothes, bear my children, and forever feel grateful and happy doing so."

That night the princess dined sumptuously on a repast of lightly sautéed frog legs swimming in a white wine and shallot cream sauce.

What Are Dogs?

FACTS:

Dogs lie around sprawled on the most comfortable piece of furniture in the house.
They do disgusting things with their mouths and then try to give you a kiss.
They are great at begging.
They leave their toys everywhere.
They growl when they're angry.
When you want to play, they want to play.
When you want to be alone, they want to play.
They will love you forever if you rub their tummies.
They can look dumb and lovable all at the same time.
They can hear a package of food opening half a block away but don't hear you when you're in the same room.

Conclusion - Dogs are tiny little men in cheap fur coats.

Women's Wisdom...

Why is it that a two-pound box of candy makes a woman gain five pounds?

Blessed are those who hunger and thirst, for they are sticking to their diets.

Sometimes I think I understand everything, then I regain consciousness.

Life is an endless struggle, full of frustrations and challenges,
but eventually you find a hairstylist you like.

I finally got my head together, and my body fell apart.

Time may be a great healer, but it's also a lousy beautician.

Brain cells come and brain cells go, but fat cells live forever.

Age doesn't always bring wisdom. Sometimes age comes alone.

Just when I was getting used to yesterday, along came today.

If at first you don't succeed, see if the loser gets anything.

You don't stop laughing because you grow old;
you grow old because you stop laughing.

Amazing! You just hang something in your closet for a while,
and it shrinks two sizes.

I don't mind the rat race, but I could do with a little more cheese.

I had to give up jogging for my health. My thighs kept rubbing together
and setting my pantyhose on fire.

It is bad to suppress laughter; it goes back down and spreads to your hips.

Can it be a mistake that "STRESSED" is "DESSERTS" spelled backwards?

Inside some of us is a thin person struggling to get out, but she can usually be
sedated with a few pieces of chocolate.

Great Wish!

Three guys are having a relaxing day fishing. Out of the blue they catch a mermaid, who begs to be set free in return for granting each of them a wish. Now one of the guys just doesn't believe it, and says:

"Ok, if you can really grant wishes, then double my I.Q."

The mermaid says, "Done."

Suddenly, the guy starts reciting Shakespeare flawlessly and analyzing it with extreme insight.

The second guy is so amazed he says to the mermaid, "Triple my I.Q." The mermaid says, "Done."

The guy starts to spout out all the mathematical solutions to problems that have been stumping all the scientists of varying fields—physics, chemistry, biology, etc.

The last guy is so enthralled with the changes in his friends that he says to the mermaid, "Quintuple my I.Q."

The mermaid looks at him and says, "You know, I normally don't try to change people's minds when they make a wish, but I advise you to reconsider."

"Nope, I want you to increase my I.Q. times five." And he threatens, "If you don't, I won't set you free."

"Please," says the mermaid "You don't know what you're asking. It'll change your entire view on the universe. Ask for something else—a million dollars, anything."

Alas, no matter what the mermaid says, the guy insists on having his I.Q. increased five times. So the mermaid sighs and pronounces:

"Done."

And he becomes a woman.

R.I.P.

Some time after Sidney died, his widow, Tillie, was finally able to speak about what a thoughtful and wonderful man her late husband had been.

"Sidney thought of everything," she told friends. "Just before he died, he called me to his bedside and handed me three envelopes. 'Tillie,' he said, 'I have put my last wishes into these three envelopes. After I'm dead, open them, and do exactly as I have instructed. Then I can rest in peace.'" "What was in the envelopes?" her friends asked.

"The first envelope contained $5,000 with a note saying, 'Please use this money to buy a nice casket.' So I bought a beautiful mahogany casket with such a soft lining that I know Sidney is resting very comfortably."

"The second envelope contained $10,000 with a note stating, 'Please use this for a nice funeral.' I arranged Sidney a very dignified funeral and bought all his favorite foods for everyone attending." "And the third envelope?" asked her friends. "The third envelope contained $25,000 with a note, 'Please use this to buy a nice stone.'"

Holding her hand in the air, Tillie said, "So, how do you like his stone?" showing off her huge new diamond ring.

Ladies Night Out...

The other day some of my friends and I went to this Ladies Night Club. One of the girls wanted to impress us, so she pulled out a $10 bill. The "dancer" came over to us, and my friend licked the $10 and stuck it to the cheek of his ass.

Not to be outdone, another friend pulled out a $20 bill. She called the guy back over, licked the $20 bill, and stuck it to his other butt cheek.

Attempting to impress the rest of us, another friend pulled out a $50 bill. She called the guy back over again, licked the $50 bill, and stuck it on his butt.

Now the attention focused on me. What could I do to top that?

So I opened my wallet and let the financial analyst in me take over. I got out my ATM card, swiped it down the crack of his ass, grabbed the $80 bucks, and went home.

Great Female Comebacks

Man: Haven't we met before?
Woman: Yes, I'm the receptionist at the VD Clinic.

Man: Haven't I seen you someplace before?
Woman: Yeah, that's why I don't go there anymore.

Man: Is this seat empty?
Woman: Yes, and this one will be too if you sit down.

Man: Hey, come on, we're both here at this bar for the same reason.
Woman: Yeah! Let's go pick up some chicks.

Man: So, wanna go back to my place?
Woman: Well, I don't know. Will two people fit under a rock?

Man: How do you like your eggs in the morning?
Woman: Unfertilized!

Man: I'm here to fulfill your every sexual fantasy.
Woman: You mean you've got both a donkey and a Great Dane?

Man: If I could see you naked, I'd die happy.
Woman: Yeah, but if I saw you naked, I'd probably die laughing.

Man: Your body is like a temple.
Woman: Sorry, there are no services today.

Man: So what do you do for a living?
Woman: I'm a female impersonator.

Man: What sign were you born under?
Woman: No Parking.

Man: Hey, baby, what's your sign?
Woman: Do not Enter.

Man: I know how to please a woman.
Woman: Then please leave me alone.

Man: Your place or mine?
Woman: Both. You go to yours, and I'll go to mine.

Man: I want to give myself to you.
Woman: I don't accept cheap gifts.

Eve and Adam...

One day in the Garden of Eden, Eve calls out to God, "Lord, I have a problem!"

"What's the problem, Eve?" comes the reply from above.

"Lord, I know you've created me and have provided this beautiful garden and all of these wonderful animals, and that hilarious comedy snake, but I'm just not happy."

"Why is that, Eve?"

"Lord, I'm lonely. And I'm sick to death of apples."

"Well, Eve, in that case, I have a solution. I shall create a man for you."

"What's a man, Lord?"

"This man will be a flawed creature with aggressive tendencies, an enormous ego, and an inability to empathize or listen to you properly. All in all, he'll give you a hard time. But, he'll be bigger and faster and more muscular than you. He'll be really good at fighting and kicking a ball about and hunting fleet-footed ruminants, and not altogether bad in the sack."

"Sounds great," says Eve, with an ironically raised eyebrow.

"Yeah, well. He's better than a poke in the eye with a burnt stick. But, you can have him on one condition."

"What's that, Lord?"

"You'll have to let him believe I made him first."

Favorite T-Shirt Lines...

GUYS HAVE FEELINGS TOO. BUT LIKE WHO CARES?

WARNING: I HAVE AN ATTITUDE AND I KNOW HOW TO USE IT.

WHY DO PEOPLE WITH CLOSED MINDS ALWAYS OPEN THEIR MOUTHS?

DON'T PISS ME OFF!
I'M RUNNING OUT OF PLACES TO HIDE THE BODIES.

REMEMBER MY NAME...YOU'LL BE SCREAMING IT LATER.

PLEASE DON'T MAKE ME KILL YOU.

AND YOUR POINT IS?

NEXT MOOD SWING: 6 MINUTES.

I'M BUSY. YOU'RE UGLY. HAVE A NICE DAY.

I HATE EVERYBODY, AND YOU'RE NEXT.

YOU KNOW YOU WANT ME.

DON'T WORRY. IT'LL ONLY SEEM KINKY THE FIRST TIME...

I'M MULTITALENTED:
I CAN TALK AND PISS YOU OFF AT THE SAME TIME.

YOU, ME, WHIPPED CREAM, HANDCUFFS. ANY QUESTIONS?

YOU HAVE THE RIGHT TO REMAIN SILENT, SO PLEASE SHUT UP.

ALL STRESSED OUT AND NO ONE TO CHOKE.

I'M ONE OF THOSE BAD THINGS THAT HAPPENS TO GOOD PEOPLE.

HOW CAN I MISS YOU IF YOU WON'T GO AWAY?

SORRY IF I LOOKED INTERESTED. I'M NOT.

IF WE ARE WHAT WE EAT, I'M FAST, CHEAP, AND EASY.

NOBODY KNOWS I'M NOT WEARING UNDERWEAR.

CIA Assassin...

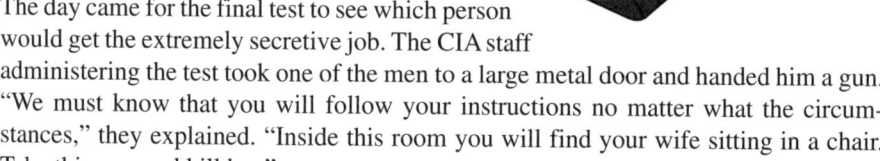

A few months ago there was an opening in the CIA for an assassin. These highly classified positions are hard to fill. Applicants have to go through a lot of testing and background checks before being considered for the position. After weeks of work the CIA narrowed the choices to two men and a woman.

The day came for the final test to see which person would get the extremely secretive job. The CIA staff administering the test took one of the men to a large metal door and handed him a gun. "We must know that you will follow your instructions no matter what the circumstances," they explained. "Inside this room you will find your wife sitting in a chair. Take this gun and kill her."

The man got a shocked look on his face and said, "You can't be serious! I could never shoot my own wife!" The CIA man concluded, "You're definitely not the right man for this job."

So they brought the second man to the same door and handed him a gun. "We must know that you will follow instructions no matter what the circumstances," they explained to the second man. "Inside you will find your wife sitting in a chair. Take this gun and kill her." The second man looked shocked. Nevertheless, he took the gun and went into the room.

All was quiet for about five minutes, then the door opened. The man came out of the room with tears in his eyes. "I tried to shoot her, but I just couldn't pull the trigger. I guess I'm not the right man for the job." "No," the CIA man replied, "You don't have what it takes. Take your wife and go home."

Only the woman was left to test. They lead her to the door and handed her the gun. "We must be sure you will follow instructions. This is your final test. Inside you will find your husband sitting in a chair. Take this gun and kill him." The woman took the gun and opened the door. Before the door even closed, the CIA men heard the gun firing all 13 shots. Then all hell broke loose in the room. They heard screaming, crashing, banging on the walls. This went on for several minutes, then all went quiet.

The door opened slowly, and there stood the woman. She wiped the blood from her brow saying, "You guys didn't tell me the gun was loaded with blanks! I had to beat him to death with the chair!"

A Bird in the Hand...

One morning while making breakfast a man walked up to his wife, pinched her on her butt, and said "You know, if you firmed this up, we could get rid of your girdle." While his remark was on the edge of intolerable, she thought better of replying and kept silent.

The next morning the man woke his wife with a pinch on the breast and said, "You know, if you firmed these up, we could get rid of your bra."

This remark deserved a response, so she rolled over and grabbed him by the penis. With a death grip in place, she said, "You know, if you firmed this up, we could get rid of your brother."

I'm not getting older. I'm getting bitter.

I DIDN'T DRIVE MY HUSBAND CRAZY. I FLEW HIM THERE. IT WAS FASTER.

The average woman would rather have beauty than brains because the average man can see better than he can think.

Seen on a feminist's T-shirt: I have PMS and a handgun.

I'M NOT 50. I'M 18 WITH 32 YEARS OF EXPERIENCE.

Just give me chocolate, and nobody gets hurt.

Are those your eyeballs? I found them in my cleavage.

I want it all, and I want it delivered.

Real women don't have hot flashes.
They have power surges.

Not all men are annoying. Some are dead.

Whisper my favorite words...."I'll buy it for you."

For Women Only...

Why did God put men on earth?
Because vibrators can't mow the lawn.

Why do men become smarter during sex?
Because they are plugged into a genius.

Why don't women have men's brains?
Because they don't have penises to put them in.

Why were men given larger brains than dogs?
So they won't hump women's legs at cocktail parties.

Why did God make men before women?
He needed a rough draft to perfect the final copy.

Why is a man's pee yellow and his sperm white?
So he can tell if he's coming or going.

Why do men snore when they lie on their backs?
Because their balls fall over their assholes,
which causes vapor lock.

What do electric trains and breasts have in common?
They're both intended for children, but
men usually end up playing with them.

Fun Weekend On The Cape...

Two young women coworkers from New York City are headed to Cape Cod for a long weekend vacation.

One says, "I'm going to eat lobster. I haven't had my fill in such a long time."

The other answers thoughtfully, "I'm not going to eat lobster. I'm going up to get scrod."

"My," replies the first girl, "I never knew the other form of that verb."

A Feminist's View Of Men...

Q: What's a man's idea of a romantic evening?
A: A candlelit football stadium.

Q: What happens when a man opens his zipper?
A: His brains fall out.

Q: What would get your man to put down the toilet seat?
A: A sex-change operation.

Q: What's the difference between a man and a chimpanzee?
A: One is hairy and smelly and always scratching it's rear;
the other's a chimpanzee.

Q. What's the difference between a man and childbirth?
A. One can be unbearably painful. The other is just having a baby.

Q: What do men and sperm have in common?
A: Both have a one-in-a-million chance of becoming human.

Q: How can you tell when a man wants sex?
A: He's breathing.

Q: How can you tell when a man's had an orgasm?
A: You can hear him snoring.

Q. What does a man consider a seven-course meal?
A. A pizza and a six pack.

Q. Why is psychoanalysis quicker for men than for women?
A. When it's time to go back to childhood, he's already there.

Q. What do most men think Mutual Orgasm is?
A. An insurance company.

Q. Why are all dumb blonde jokes one-liners?
A. So men can remember them.

Chaos, panic, and disorder—my work here is done!

It Takes A Lot Of Strength
To Find 1000 Good Jokes

Everyone said it would be fun. Almost everyone thought it would be easy. No one suggested it might be hard work. Putting this new joke book together has been all of those, and more.

Filling the days reading funny stories is a great deal more entertaining than most jobs. Over the past year I have realized Internet jokes have a predictable life. A new joke flashes onto the screen, quickly followed by near or exact duplicates in a few hours or days. Over the next month the same joke may recycle once a week. After a year it returns about once a month. Then it disappears.

Jokes From The Internet is a new venture. For 35 years I traveled the world as a magazine photojournalist. Twenty-eight of those were spent mainly writing and photographing articles for *National Geographic*. Despite scores of scientific and environmental articles, I am best known for the 14-year gemstone series I created for *Geographic*. As an outgrowth of that work, I became a Graduate Gemologist and formed Gem Book Publishers to publish what has become America's most popular gem book series. Now I write and consult extensively on gemstones and locate rare gems for clients who love exotic treasures.

Just as my ongoing nine-book series of gem books is much more satisfying and useful than a single volume, I believe the idea of a continuing series of *Jokes From The Internet* will find its place among American humor books. I invite you to participate. Below you will find the ways to contact me. When you have a joke or story you think is funny, please send it to me so I can share it with the world. I hope you have some good laughs every day from this happy project. Thanks.

Fred Ward

fward@erols.com
http://www.erols.com/fward
Telephone: 301-983-1990
FAX: 301-983-3980

If errors have been made, others will be blamed!